10 REASONS

Why I Hate

CHRISTIAN DATING

How Anyone Can Go From Cultural to Kingdom Dating

ACKNOWLEDGEMENTS

I want to give special thanks to God and acknowledge the wisdom and guidance from the Bible, particularly which has been a source of strength and inspiration throughout this journey. Without the truth of Scripture, this book would not have been possible.

I would like to extend my deepest gratitude to my spiritual parents, Apostle Tony Wade and Prophetess Felecia Wade. Your unwavering love, guidance, and leadership have been a cornerstone in my life. Your wisdom, example of excellence and mentorship have shaped me not only as a person but as a leader. Words can not express how much I appreciate you. This book is a reflection of the seeds you've sown in my life. Thank you for consistently showing me what it means to walk in faith, purpose, and grace. I am eternally grateful for your impact and the way you have empowered and loved my family and I.

I want to take a moment to acknowledge and express my heartfelt gratitude to everyone in the community who played a role in my journey from being a homeless single mom to where I stand today. Your support, encouragement, and kindness have been invaluable, and I am forever thankful for each person who offered a helping hand, a word of encouragement, or simply believed in me when the road seemed hardest. This book is a testament to the power of community, faith, and perseverance, and I am deeply grateful for all of you who helped me rise and walk in my purpose.

I want to give special recognition to my daughter, Nadia, who walked with me through every step of this journey. You were by my side through it all, and your strength and resilience have been a source of inspiration for me. Nadia, I am so incredibly proud of the young woman you are becoming. Your love and support mean the world to me, and I am blessed beyond measure to be your mommy.

CONTENTS

INTRODUCTION...1

Chapter 1

I HATE HOW CULTURAL DATING PRESSURES YOU TO CONFORM.................4

Chapter 2

I HATE TEMPORARY RELATIONSHIPS THAT ONLY LEAD TO HEARTBREAK 10

Chapter 3

I HATE HOW IGNORING GOD'S PLAN IN DATING CAUSES UNNECESSARY COMPLICATIONS...26

Chapter 4

I HATE HOW WE OVERLY INVEST IN DATING – THE DANGERS OF OVER-INVESTING IN RELATIONSHIPS 34

Chapter 5

I HATE THAT SO MANY BOUNDARIES HAVE BEEN BLURRED AND CROSSED 42

Chapter 6

I HATE THAT SO MANY PEOPLE ARE FAKE CHRISTIANS 59

Chapter 7

I HATE CHRISTIAN DATING BECAUSE OF THE PRESSURES OF PURITY CULTURE 69

Chapter 8

I HATE THAT WE DO NOT KNOW HOW TO HAVE REAL RELATIONSHIPS BECAUSE OF TRAUMA AND UNHEALED WOUNDS 77

Chapter 9

I HATE HOW FALSE EXPECTATIONS AND FANTASIES CAUSE SELF-DECEPTION AND BLINDNESS TO RED FLAGS 87

Chapter 10

I HATE HOW ONCE PEOPLE START DATING, THEY BEGIN TO NEGLECT FRIENDSHIPS AND COMMUNITY 95

Conclusion

LET GOD LEAD YOUR RELATIONSHIPS, AND TRUST HIS PLAN 103

NOTES 111

INTRODUCTION

When I stop to think about **Christian dating**, the first thing that comes to mind is confusion. So many of us are told to date differently, to follow biblical principles, and to stay pure, but the **world's culture** has crept into the church and made dating feel like a game. I've seen it firsthand. We're bombarded with mixed messages from the church, social media, and our friends. We're pressured to conform to the world's standards of dating, and somewhere along the way, the **Kingdom of God perspective** on relationships gets lost.

Let me be honest with you. I hate what Christian dating has turned into. It feels like we're caught between two worlds—trying to follow God's way but still being influenced by the world's way. There's pressure to look a certain way, to act a certain way, and to find "the one" as if marriage is the ultimate goal of our faith. But let me tell you something: **dating is not the goal—Jesus is.**

For years, I did things the world's way. I thought I could write my own love story, make my own decisions, and somehow still end up with God's best. I convinced myself that I knew better, and I paid the price for it. My life was derailed. I became a single mom because of my choices, and I hurt my daughter in the process. No matter how much I tried to explain, she still had to live with the consequences of my decisions. That was a heavy burden to carry, and for many years, I felt like I had ruined my chances of having a godly relationship. I completely counted myself out.

But here's the beautiful thing about God—**He is a Redeemer**. He took my broken pieces, my mistakes, and my failures, and He made something beautiful out of my life. I had to learn how to **repent**, how to stop doing things my way, and how to trust Him completely. And when I finally surrendered, He wrote a love story for me that I couldn't have imagined. Today, I'm happily married to a man who loves Jesus with all his heart, and we have five amazing children together. But I'll tell you right now—this is all God's doing.

This book isn't about **10 easy steps** to finding a spouse or a magical formula for perfect relationships. This is about getting back to the **heart of God's plan** for dating and relationships. It's about going from **cultural dating**—which is based on worldly ideas and temporary pleasures—to **Kingdom dating**, which is rooted in God's Word and His eternal purpose for your life.

So why do I hate Christian dating? Because so much of what we call "Christian dating" today isn't even Christian. It's cultural. We've brought the world's standards into the church, and we're trying to fit God into our plans instead of letting Him lead. We've made dating an idol, and we've forgotten that the most important relationship we'll ever have is our relationship with Jesus.

This book is for anyone who's tired of doing things the world's way. It's for those of you who want more out of your relationships—who want to experience God's best. Whether you're single, dating, or even engaged, this book will help you understand how to shift from cultural dating to Kingdom dating. It's time to stop conforming to the world's patterns and start letting God write your love story.

If you're ready to stop chasing what the world offers and start seeking God's plan for your love life, then let's dive in. Together, we'll explore the **10 reasons** why I hate Christian dating as it stands today and how we can move from confusion and compromise to clarity and commitment in our relationships. Trust me, when you let God lead, He'll take you places you never imagined.

I HATE HOW CULTURAL DATING PRESSURES YOU TO CONFORM

Have you ever felt like you needed to change who you are just to fit into the dating scene? Or maybe you've felt the pressure to hurry up and get into a relationship because "everyone else" is doing it. This is the trap of cultural dating. The world sets up a system that pushes us to conform, but the truth is, God's plan for relationships doesn't look anything like what the culture tells us. In fact, it's COMPLETELY Different.

THERE IS NO SUCH THING AS CHRISTIAN DATING IN THE BIBLE

Let's start with a bold statement: There is no such thing as "Christian dating." Yes, you read that right. Nowhere in the Bible will you find instructions on how to date. In fact, the entire concept of dating, as we know it today, didn't exist in biblical times. The Bible speaks of marriage, of courting, of relationships, but it never describes the modern-day practices of casual dating, swiping left or right, or hanging out "just to see where it goes."

Instead, God calls us to a much higher standard—one that centers on Him, not on cultural norms. Matthew 6:33 says, "Seek first the kingdom of God and His righteousness, and all these things shall be added to you." This applies to everything in our lives, including dating. When we put God first, everything else—our relationships, our future spouse—will come in His perfect time.

But the pressure is real, right? Society says that if you're not in a relationship by a certain age or if you're not experiencing certain things—like going on dates every weekend or being engaged by 25—then you're somehow behind. We live in a world where social media feeds are flooded with happy couples, engagement photos, and wedding announcements. It's easy to feel like you need to "catch up." But God calls us to trust Him with the details of our lives, including our love story.

CULTURAL DATING PRESSURES: THE LIES WE BELIEVE

Let's unpack some of the common lies that cultural dating tells us:

"YOU HAVE TO BE IN A RELATIONSHIP TO BE HAPPY"

The world tells us that being single means something is wrong with us, or that happiness is only found in romantic relationships. But this is a lie. Our joy should come from our relationship with God first. Psalm 16:11 says, "In your presence, there is fullness of joy." Fullness of joy—not a piece of joy, not just enough joy to get by, but *fullness* of joy—is found in God, not in a boyfriend or girlfriend. A relationship is a gift from God, not a source of identity or self-worth.

"IF YOU'RE NOT DATING, YOU'RE MISSING OUT"

The culture pushes us to believe that we are somehow missing out on life if we're not dating or constantly in a relationship. But this idea is based on fear—the fear of being left behind, the fear of loneliness, and the fear of not fitting in. But 2 Timothy 1:7 tells us, "For God gave us a spirit not of fear but of power and love and self-control." We don't have to give in to the fear of missing out. God has a unique plan for each of us, and rushing into relationships will only pull us away from that plan.

"IT'S OKAY TO COMPROMISE YOUR VALUES TO GET INTO OR STAY IN A RELATIONSHIP"

One of the most dangerous lies of cultural dating is that it's okay to let go of some of your standards in order to fit in. Maybe you feel pressure to date someone who doesn't share your faith, or maybe you've been tempted to lower your boundaries to keep a relationship going. The Bible specifically tells us, "To not conform to this world, but be transformed by the renewing of your mind" (Romans 12:2). Compromise may feel like an easier path in the moment, but it leads to heartache. As Kingdom citizens we are called to stand firm in our faith and trust Him to bring the right person into our lives, even if it means waiting.

BREAKING FREE FROM CULTURAL CONFORMITY

So how do we break free from the pressures of cultural dating? The answer is simple, yet challenging: we need to shift our focus from the world's standards to God's standards. Let's look at three practical ways to do this:

SEEK GOD'S APPROVAL, NOT THE WORLD'S

It's easy to get caught up in wanting to fit in with what everyone else is doing, but Galatians 1:10 reminds us, "For, am I now seeking the approval of man or God? Or am I attempting to please the man? If I were still seeking to please people, I would not be a servant of Christ." In our relationships, our primary goal should be to please God, not to meet the expectations of society. When you're dating, ask yourself: Does this relationship honor God? Is this what He wants for me?

BE PATIENT AND TRUST GOD'S TIMING

One of the biggest pressures we face is the idea that we have to be in a relationship right now. But Isaiah 40:31 promises, "They who wait for the Lord shall renew their strength; they shall mount up with wings like eagles; they shall run and not be weary; they shall walk and not faint." Waiting is hard, but it's worth it. God is not in a rush, and He has the perfect timing for your love story. Don't settle for less just because you feel like you're waiting too long.

SURROUND YOURSELF WITH GODLY INFLUENCES

The people you surround yourself with will either push you toward God or pull you away from Him. Proverbs 13:20 says,

"Walk with the wise and become wise, for a companion of fools suffers harm." When it comes to dating, seek out friends and mentors will encourage you to follow God's standards, even when it's hard. Surround yourself with friends who remind you that your worth comes from Christ, not a relationship.

LET'S LOOK AT DANIEL

Think about Daniel from the Bible. He lived in a culture that pressured him to conform to the ways of the world. He was surrounded by people who ate food that was forbidden, worshiped false gods, and lived in ways that dishonored God. But Daniel didn't give in. Daniel 1:8 tells us, "But Daniel resolved not to defile himself with the royal food and wine." Daniel chose to honor God, even when it would have been easier to follow the crowd.

We need to be like Daniel in our dating lives. We need to resolve not to defile ourselves with the ways of the world. Just because the culture says it's okay doesn't mean it's okay for us. God calls us to be set apart (1 Peter 2:9).

Don't let the world define your worth or your relationship goals. Cultural dating will push you to conform, but God calls you to stand out. He has a plan for your life that is far better than anything the world can offer. Stop listening to the lies of the culture, and start seeking God's plan for your relationships.

TIME OF REFLECTION

Write down one area of your dating life that makes you feel pressured to conform to the world's standards. Pray about it, asking God to help you break free from that pressure. Then, make a commitment to seek His will in that area. Whether it's your boundaries, your expectations, or your timing, trust that God's way is better than the world's.

In this first chapter, we've tackled the pressure to conform to cultural dating. But there's so much more to unpack as we dive deeper into the reasons why cultural dating leads to heartbreak and confusion. The next chapter will focus on the problem of temporary relationships that distract us from God's purpose for our lives. Stay tuned!

Chapter 2

I HATE TEMPORARY RELATIONSHIPS THAT ONLY LEAD TO HEARTBREAK

Cultural dating often leads to situations without labels and brief romances. You meet someone, feel a spark, and start dating. For a while, everything is exciting and new. But soon, that thrill fades. The relationship, once so promising, falls apart. You're left with heartbreak, confusion, and sometimes even regret. Why? Because the relationship was built on attraction, emotions, and temporary feelings rather than something deeper—Kingdom compatibility.

In this chapter, we'll dive deeper into the problem of temporary relationships and why they often lead to heartbreak. We'll also explore what it means to shift from focusing on attraction and surface-level compatibility to seeking Kingdom compatibility—the kind of relationship that is built on a foundation of shared faith, purpose, and a desire to glorify God.

WHY TEMPORARY RELATIONSHIPS DON'T LAST

Temporary relationships are just that—temporary. They're often built on things that fade over time, like physical attraction, excitement, or a desire to not be alone. These kinds of relationships can feel exhilarating in the beginning, but they lack the depth and foundation needed to sustain them long-term.

Attraction Fades Over Time: Physical attraction is a wonderful thing, and it's natural to be drawn to someone based on their appearance or charm. However, Proverbs 31:30 gives us a sobering reminder: "Charm is deceptive, and beauty is fleeting; but a woman who fears the Lord is to be praised." This verse isn't just about women—men, too, can fall into the trap of relying on charm and good looks to sustain a relationship. The truth is, physical appearance changes over time, and attraction alone isn't enough to build a lasting relationship.

When we base our relationships primarily on physical attraction, we're setting ourselves up for disappointment. Once the initial excitement fades, we're left with the reality that we don't know this person deeply enough. We may realize that we have little in common, or worse, that they're not aligned with our values and beliefs.

Emotions are Unreliable: Temporary relationships often rely heavily on emotions—how someone makes us feel in the moment. But emotions can be fickle. They can change from day to day, or even moment to moment. One day you might feel deeply in love, and the next, you might be questioning whether this person is right for you. Jeremiah 17:9 warns us, "The heart is deceitful above all things and beyond cure. Who can understand it?"

Emotions are not a reliable guide for making decisions and especially not when it comes to relationships. If we base our choices on fleeting feelings, we'll find ourselves in a cycle of starting and ending relationships, always chasing the next emotional high but never finding anything lasting or fulfilling.

Lack of Purpose Leads to Confusion: Many temporary relationships are marked by a lack of clear purpose. The world often tells us that dating is just for fun or to pass the time, but without a clear purpose, these relationships can quickly become confusing. Are you dating just because you're bored or lonely? Are you in this relationship because you feel pressure from others to be in one? When we enter relationships without intentionality, we risk wasting time, energy, and emotions on something that was never meant to last.

God's design for relationships is intentional. In Genesis 2:24, God says, "That is why a man leaves his father and mother and is united to his wife, and they become one flesh." This verse reminds us that our ultimate purpose of a romantic relationship should be marriage—a lifelong covenant. Temporary relationships that lack this kind of purpose often leave us feeling lost and unsure of where we stand with the other person.

KINGDOM COMPATIBILITY: THE FOUNDATION OF LASTING RELATIONSHIPS

Some of you may be asking, if temporary relationships are so problematic, what should we be focusing on instead? The answer is Kingdom compatibility. This means seeking a partner who shares your faith, values, and commitment to following God's plan for your lives. Rather than focusing solely on attraction or how someone makes you feel, you should be asking deeper questions about whether this person is spiritually aligned with you.

WHAT DOES KINGDOM COMPATIBILITY LOOK LIKE?

A Shared Faith in Christ: The most important factor in Kingdom compatibility is that both partners share a deep, genuine faith in Jesus Christ. 2 Corinthians 6:14 tells us, "Do not be unequally yoked with unbelievers. For what partnership has righteousness with lawlessness? Or what fellowship has light with darkness?" This doesn't mean you're looking for someone who just goes to church or says they're a Christian. It means you're seeking someone who has a vibrant relationship with God and is committed to growing in their faith.

A shared faith provides the core foundation for every other aspect of the relationship. When both people are seeking God first, they are more likely to approach their relationship with humility, love, and a desire to honor God in everything they do. They're also more likely to rely on prayer, Scripture, and godly counsel to guide them through the challenges of life.

Aligned Values and Life Goals: Kingdom compatibility also means that you and your partner share similar values and life goals. This includes things like how you view marriage, family, and ministry. Amos 3:3 asks, "Do two walk together unless they have agreed to do so?" In other words, you need to be walking in the same direction, pursuing the same goals in life, if you want your relationship to thrive.

For example, if one person feels called to be a missionary in another country while the other feels called to stay and serve in their local community, that could create tension. Or if one person values financial security above all else, while the other feels called to a lifestyle of generosity and simplicity, that could lead to conflict. Being Kingdom-compatible means that you're aligned not just spiritually, but in your vision for the future. While dating do not forget that this is your interview phase! I know they are cute but don't allow the attraction and rushing to get married to prevent you from asking the questions that truly matter.

Mutual Encouragement in Spiritual Growth: A Kingdom-compatible relationship is one where both partners encourage each other to grow closer to God. Hebrews 10:24 reminds us, "And let us consider how we may spur one another on toward love and good deeds." In a Christ-centered relationship, you're not just focused on each other—you're focused on helping each other become more like Christ.

This kind of relationship includes praying for one another, faithfully studying the Bible, allowing the Holy Spirit to lead and guide you, and challenging each other to live out your faith in everyday life. When both partners are committed to growing spiritually individually, the relationship becomes a place where you can sharpen each other and draw closer to God.

THE COST OF BEING UNEQUALLY YOKED

Many people think it's okay to date someone who doesn't share their faith, as long as the person is kind or fun to be around. If this is you, YOU ARE ABOUT TO MAKE A HUGE MISTAKE! Being unequally yoked can and will lead to a lot of heartache down the road.

1. How can two walk together less they agree?
2. What does light and darkness have in common?

If you chose to walk into a relationship knowingly with an unbeliever, know that you are completely opening yourself up to so many things. The Kingdom of our God and the Kingdom of darkness cannot coexist. When you enter into these kinds of relationships it will ultimately cause frustration, tension, and even lead to compromising your own beliefs and values.

Imagine two oxen yoked together, but one is stronger or pulling in a different direction. The weaker ox will struggle, and the two won't be able to move forward together. In the same way, if you're in a relationship with someone who isn't spiritually aligned with you, it can feel like you're constantly struggling to keep the relationship on track. You might end up compromising your faith, lowering your standards, or feeling spiritually drained.

THE BREAKDOWN OF BEING A CHRISTIAN DATING AN UNBELIEVER: WHY IT LEADS TO HEARTACHE ACCORDING TO SCRIPTURE

Dating is a beautiful process when it's aligned with God's will, but when a Christian dates an unbeliever, there's an unavoidable clash of values, beliefs, and life goals. This breakdown isn't just theoretical—it's biblical. Scripture warns us repeatedly about being "unequally yoked" and shows the consequences of forming intimate relationships with those who don't share our faith. Let's take a deeper dive into why dating an unbeliever leads to spiritual, emotional, and relational breakdowns, and what God says about it.

UNEQUALLY YOKED: A BIBLICAL WARNING

The idea of being "unequally yoked" comes from 2 Corinthians 6:14-16, where the Apostle Paul writes: **"Do not be unequally yoked with unbelievers. For what partnership has righteousness with lawlessness? Or what fellowship has light with darkness? What harmony is there between Christ and Belial? Or what does a believer have in common with an unbeliever?"**

This passage gives a clear warning to Christians: Do not form partnerships, especially intimate ones like romantic relationships, with unbelievers. The expression "unequally yoked" is derived from farming. In ancient times, two animals—typically oxen—were yoked together with a wooden bar to plow a field. For the process to work, both animals needed to be of equal strength and purpose, moving in the same direction. If they weren't, the work would become impossible.

They would constantly struggle against each other, pulling in different directions.

Similarly, in a relationship, if you are yoked with someone who doesn't share your faith and values, you'll constantly struggle. While you're trying to move toward God, they're moving in a completely different direction, leading to frustration, unnecessary conflicts which ultimately leads to a breakdown in the relationship. Let's go deeper into this.

CONFLICTING FOUNDATIONS

The biggest issue in dating an unbeliever is that you and your partner are standing on different foundations. There are two different Kingdoms at play in this situation, the Kingdom of our God and the Kingdom of darkness. As a Christian, your life is built on Christ, and your purpose is to glorify God in all that you do. But for an unbeliever, their life is not centered on Christ. Their values, goals, and worldview are different.

Jesus speaks about the importance of a strong foundation in Matthew 7:24-27. He says:

"Therefore, everyone who hears these words of mine and puts them into practice is like a wise man who built his house on the rock. The rain came down, the streams rose, and the winds blew and beat against that house; yet it did not fall, because it had its foundation on the rock. But everyone who hears these words of mine and does not put

them into practice is like a foolish man who built his house on sand. The rain came down, the streams rose, and the winds blew and beat against that house, and it fell with a great crash."

When a Christian dates an unbeliever, they are essentially trying to build a relationship where one person's foundation is on the rock (Christ) and the other's is on the sand (the world). When storms come—when challenges arise in the relationship, when moral decisions need to be made, or when life's difficulties hit—there will be a crash. One person will be relying on their faith in God, while the other may be relying on their own wisdom or worldly ideas. This only causes tension, frustration, and heartbreak. The relationship is not built on a united Kingdom and a strong foundation.

DIFFERENT PRIORITIES AND VALUES

Another major breakdown in dating an unbeliever is the clash of priorities and values. As Christians, we are called to live according to the Word of God, and that shapes every part of our lives—our time, finances, how we treat others, and our purpose in life. An unbeliever, however, doesn't live by the same standard. They may have good intentions, but their worldview is not shaped by Scripture.

Jesus teaches us in Matthew 6:33: **"But seek first the kingdom of God and His righteousness, and all these things will be added to you."** As a Christian, your priority is to seek God's kingdom first, above all else. But for someone who doesn't share that priority, their focus might be on other things—

success, material wealth, personal happiness, or other worldly goals. Imagine trying to make decisions as a couple when you have such different priorities. One person might want to serve in ministry, while the other person sees that as a waste of time. One person wants to pursue purity, while the other person wants to have sex. One might believe in tithing and being generous. The other aims for financial security or the experience of worldly pleasures. Over time, these differences in priorities will create tension and lead to compromise. You might have to give up your beliefs and spiritual goals to keep the peace in the relationship.

This is exactly why God warns us in 1 Corinthians 15:33: **"Do not be deceived: 'Bad company ruins good morals.'"** When you're yoked to someone who doesn't share your faith, their influence can lead you away from God's purpose for your life.

LACK OF SPIRITUAL LEADERSHIP

In a Kingdom relationship, spiritual leadership is crucial, especially for the man. Ephesians 5:25-26 instructs husbands to lead their wives in a Christ-like manner: **"Husbands, love your wives, just as Christ loved the church and gave himself up for her to make her holy, cleansing her by the washing with water through the word."**

In a Christian marriage or serious relationship, the man is called to lead his wife and family spiritually, just as Christ leads the Church. But if a Christian woman is dating an unbeliever, he cannot provide the spiritual leadership she needs because he doesn't know Christ himself. A woman might find herself spiritually isolated in the relationship, unable to share the most important part of her life—her faith—with the person she's supposed to be closest to.

For Christian men dating unbelievers, the dynamic can be equally challenging. Instead of leading the relationship in a way that honors God, they might feel pressured to compromise on their spiritual values or take on all the responsibility for keeping the relationship centered on Christ. Without both partners fully committed to Jesus and spiritual growth, the relationship becomes unbalanced and ultimately breaks down.

COMPROMISING ON BIBLICAL STANDARDS

One of the most dangerous aspects of dating an unbeliever is the temptation to compromise on your faith and biblical standards. When you're in a relationship with someone who doesn't share your commitment to following God, you may find yourself lowering your standards to avoid conflict or to keep the relationship going. For example:

Purity and Boundaries: An unbeliever may not see the need for sexual purity or the importance of boundaries in the relationship. 1 Thessalonians 4:3-5 says, **"It is God's will that you should be sanctified: that you should avoid sexual immorality; that each of you should learn to control your own body in a way that is holy and honorable, not in passionate lust like the pagans, who do not know God."** If your partner doesn't value these principles, you may feel pressured to engage in sexual immorality or compromise on other areas of purity.

Discipleship and Spiritual Growth: You may find yourself spending less time in church, reading the Bible, or praying because your partner doesn't prioritize spiritual growth. Proverbs 13:20 tells us, **"Walk with the wise and become wise, for a companion of fools suffers harm."** When you're dating someone who isn't seeking God, you may be pulled away from your relationship with Him.

CONFLICT AND HEARTACHE OVER MAJOR LIFE DECISIONS

One of the most significant issues that arise when a Christian dates an unbeliever is how to handle major life decisions. Whether it's decisions about marriage, raising children, finances, or career choices, the lack of spiritual unity will become more evident over time.

For example, if you plan to have children in the future, how will you raise them? As a Christian, you'll likely want to raise your children to know and love God, to read the Bible, and to attend church. But if your partner doesn't share your faith, they might resist that idea or be indifferent to it. Amos 3:3 asks a critical question:

"HOW CAN TWO PEOPLE WALK TOGETHER UNLESS THEY AGREE?"

These disagreements can lead to long-term frustration and heartache, as you realize that the person you're with doesn't share your most deeply held convictions.

BIBLICAL EXAMPLES OF THE DANGERS OF MARRYING UNBELIEVERS

The Bible gives us several examples of how dangerous it can be to be in a relationship with someone who doesn't share your faith:

SOLOMON AND HIS FOREIGN WIVES

King Solomon started out as a wise and godly king, but as he married foreign wives who did not worship the one true God, his heart was turned away from God. 1 Kings 11:4-6 says:

"As Solomon grew old, his wives turned his heart after other gods, and his heart was not fully devoted to the Lord his God, as the heart of David his father had been. He followed Ashtoreth the goddess of the Sidonians, and Molek The detestable god of the Ammonites. So, Solomon did evil in the eyes of the Lord; he did not follow the Lord completely." Even someone as wise as Solomon fell into spiritual compromise because of his relationships with unbelieving women. Over time, these relationships led him away from God.

SAMSON AND DELILAH

Samson was called by God to be a judge and leader of Israel, but his downfall came when he became romantically involved with Delilah, a woman who did not share his faith or values. She betrayed him, leading to his capture by the Philistines (Judges 16). Samson's relationship with Delilah illustrates how dangerous it is to get involved with someone who isn't aligned with your spiritual beliefs.

GOD'S CALL FOR HOLINESS IN RELATIONSHIPS

God desires for us to be holy in every aspect of our lives, including our relationships. 1 Peter 1:15-16 says, **"But just as He who called you is holy, so be holy in all you do; for it is written: 'Be holy, because I am holy.'"** Dating and marriage are no exception to this call to holiness. When we pursue relationships with unbelievers, we risk compromising that holiness and stepping outside of God's will for our lives.

THE BREAKDOWN IS INEVITABLE

When a Christian dates an unbeliever, the relationship is fundamentally built on two different foundations. The believer's life is built on Christ, while the unbeliever's life is built on the world. There are two different kingdoms, which are the Kingdom of God and the Kingdom of darkness. Over time, these differing foundations and kingdoms will collide, causing conflict, compromise, and spiritual heartache. The Bible is clear in its warnings against being unequally yoked because God knows the breakdown that will happen when we try to form intimate relationships with those who don't share our faith.

PRACTICAL WAYS TO SEEK KINGDOM COMPATIBILITY

Now that we understand why temporary relationships are problematic and why Kingdom compatibility is essential, let's look at some practical ways you can change your focus when it comes to dating.

1. **Pray for Discernment:** One of the most important things you can do when dating is to pray for discernment. Ask God to give you wisdom and clarity as you get to know someone. James 1:5 encourages us, "If any of you lacks wisdom, you should ask God, who gives generously to all without finding fault, and it will be given to you." Before you enter a relationship, ask God to show you whether this person is truly compatible with you spiritually.

2. **Have Intentional Conversations:** Don't be afraid to ask deep questions early in the relationship. Ask about the person's relationship with God, their spiritual growth, and their vision for the future. This isn't about being too serious too soon—it's about being intentional. Proverbs 20:5 says, "The purposes of a person's heart are deep waters, but one who has insight draws them out." Don't settle for surface-level conversations. Ask the hard questions now to avoid heartbreak later.

3. **Take Your Time:** Rushing into a relationship can cause you to overlook red flags or ignore important issues. Proverbs 19:2 warns, "Desire without knowledge is not good—how much more will hasty feet miss the way!" Take your time to truly get to know the person. Don't rush to make emotional or physical commitments before you're sure that this person is aligned with God's plan for your life.

4. **Seek Godly Counsel:** Proverbs 15:22 tells us, "Plans fail for lack of counsel, but with many advisers they succeed."

Surround yourself with godly friends, mentors, or spiritual leaders who can offer advice and help you see things clearly. They can help you identify potential problems or confirm that you're on the right path. Don't be afraid to seek outside help as you navigate dating.

They may seem exciting at first. But temporary relationships will ultimately lead to heartache. They distract from God's purpose for your life. Don't settle for fleeting emotions or surface-level attraction. Instead, seek Kingdom compatibility. Save yourself the headache and choose someone who honors God in their life and in your relationship.

Chapter 3

I HATE HOW IGNORING GOD'S PLAN IN DATING CAUSES UNNECESSARY COMPLICATIONS

When we ignore God's plan for dating, things get messy, fast. This is something we all need to understand: dating wasn't meant to be a game, and it's not just for fun. God has a purpose for everything in our lives, and that includes relationships. If we don't date with His purpose in mind, we end up with complications that bring confusion, heartbreak, and spiritual compromise.

Dating the world's way may feel exciting, but it leads to dead ends when it's not rooted in God's design. Instead of building a relationship on something solid, like shared faith and purpose, cultural dating often prioritizes temporary feelings, fun, and attraction. In this chapter, we'll dive into the importance of following God's plan for dating and avoiding the pitfalls of cultural dating. We'll focus on how to ask the deep questions that help us discover if we're truly compatible with someone—not just for today, but for a lifetime of honoring God together.

Let's break this down into practical steps for both men and women as we look at God's principles for dating with purpose.

GOD'S PLAN: DATE TO MATE, NOT FOR PLAY

From the beginning, God's intention for relationships has been clear: they are meant to lead to marriage, and marriage is meant to reflect His love and covenant with us. When we date just for fun or because we're lonely, we step outside of this purpose and create unnecessary complications, confusion, and heartbreak. Genesis 2:24 lays the foundation for marriage: "That is why a man leaves his father and mother and is united to his wife, and they become one flesh." The goal of dating is to find a spouse with whom you can be united in marriage, not to pass time, fulfill temporary desires or fill those voids you should have taken to the Lord. When we understand that dating is about **finding a lifelong partner**, not just satisfying short-term emotions, we approach relationships with greater care and wisdom.

The world tells us to date for excitement, but God says to date for **commitment**. God's Word teaches us that our relationships should lead toward something meaningful, not leave us stuck in a cycle of confusion and heartbreak. Men and women alike need to approach dating with this mindset: we are **dating to mate, not to play.**

THE DANGERS OF IGNORING GOD'S PURPOSE

When we ignore God's design for dating, several complications arise:

Emotional Roller Coasters: When you date without purpose, your emotions become the driving force. One moment you're over the moon because things are going well, and the next, you're stressed and confused because you don't know where the relationship is headed. Proverbs 4:23 warns us, "Above all else, guard your heart, for everything you do flows from it." When you don't guard your heart, especially in dating, you end up emotionally drained from giving your heart away too soon, to someone who may not be God's best for you.

Emotional ups and downs happen when you date based on feelings alone. While it's great to feel excited about someone, those feelings can easily fade. If your relationship isn't built on a solid foundation of shared faith and values, the emotions will eventually wear out, leaving you confused and heartbroken.

Spiritual Drift: Ignoring God's plan can also lead to spiritual compromise. In relationships, the spiritual direction you and your partner are going matters more than anything else. 2 Corinthians 6:14 says, "Do not be yoked together with unbelievers. For what do righteousness and wickedness have in common? Or what fellowship can light have with darkness?" Dating someone who doesn't share your faith or who isn't as committed to Christ as you are will eventually pull you away from God's path.

It's really tempting to believe that you can "help them change" or lead them closer to God, but this is rarely how it works. The truth is, when your spiritual lives aren't aligned, one person is often dragged down spiritually, instead of both growing in Christ together. Compromising on your faith for the sake of a relationship can lead to losing focus on God's Purpose for your life.

Wasted Time and Energy: Dating without intention often leads to wasted time. Instead of using your time wisely to pursue God's calling for your life, you might find yourself entangled in relationships that aren't going anywhere. Ephesians 5:15-16 urges us, "Be very careful, then, how you live—not as unwise but as wise, making the most of every opportunity, because the days are evil." Every day is a gift, and God wants us to use our time wisely.

Dating without a clear purpose can eat up years of your life that could have been spent pursuing your calling, developing your spiritual gifts, or preparing for the right person God has for you. This doesn't mean dating should feel like a burden, but it should be intentional and aligned with God's plan.

FEELINGS VS. FAITH: DON'T GET DISTRACTED BY THE "WARM FUZZY" STAGE

It's easy to get swept up in the "warm fuzzy" stage of dating—the butterflies, the excitement, the thrill of something new. But feelings can be misleading. The Bible teaches us in Jeremiah 17:9, "The heart is deceitful above all things and beyond cure.

Who can understand it?" Our hearts, which are often driven by emotions, can lead us into relationships that look good on the surface but lack the depth needed for a godly, lasting relationship.

Here's the truth: feelings will come and go, but faith is the foundation that will keep a relationship strong. You need more than just chemistry to sustain a relationship for a lifetime. When challenges come (and they will), attraction and excitement won't be enough to carry you through. That's why we need to prioritize kingdom compatibility, not just emotional connection.

Instead of focusing solely on how someone makes you feel, ask yourself: **Does this relationship honor God? Are we both seeking to grow in Christ together? Is our connection rooted in faith, not just feelings?**

THE "INTERVIEW STAGE": ASK THE DEEP QUESTIONS EARLY

Now let's talk about the importance of what I call the **"interview stage"** in dating. When we meet someone, it's easy to stay on the surface. We talk about likes, dislikes, hobbies, and fun activities. But if you're serious about following God's Plan, you need to dig deeper, especially early on. This isn't just about finding out if they like the same movies or have similar tastes in food. It's about finding out if you're aligned on the big, spiritual things.

As Christians, dating should involve asking important, God-honoring questions that help you determine whether this person is someone you could marry.

Here are some examples of deep questions that you should ask during the "interview stage":

- What is your relationship with God like?
- What is your relationship with your parents like?
- Are you walking through any emotional or mental health issues?
- How do you prioritize your spiritual growth?
- What are your views on marriage and raising a family?
- How do you feel about keeping purity in a relationship?
- What are your personal goals, and do they align with God's will?
- How do you deal with conflict, and what does forgiveness mean to you?

These questions help you get to the heart of someone's character and faith. Proverbs 20:5 says, "The purposes of a person's heart are deep waters, but one who has insight draws them out." Asking these deep questions early in the relationship can save you from months or even years of heartbreak later on. It's not about being too serious too soon—it's about being **intentional**.

BIBLICAL PRINCIPLES FOR DATING WITH PURPOSE

Here are some key biblical principles to guide both men and women when dating with God's purpose in mind:

- **Seek God First (Matthew 6:33)** Jesus said, "But seek first the kingdom of God and His righteousness, and all these things will be added to you." This means that before you seek a relationship, seek God's will for your life. Let Him shape your desires, and trust Him to bring the right person into your life at the right time.

- **Stop Rushing (Ecclesiastes 3:11)** God has made everything beautiful in its time. Rushing into a relationship just because you're lonely or feel pressured by society won't lead to lasting happiness. Trust God's timing, and don't settle for something less than His best.

- **Guard Your Heart (Proverbs 4:23)** Your heart is precious to God. Be wise in who you allow to have access to it. Don't give your heart away easily, and protect your emotional and spiritual well-being by setting clear boundaries in relationships.

- **Be Equally Yoked (2 Corinthians 6:14)** If you're a believer, the person you date should be equally committed to their faith. Shared faith is the foundation of a godly relationship, and being unequally yoked will lead to spiritual tension and conflict.

- **Focus on Character, Not Just Chemistry (Proverbs 31:30)** "Charm is deceitful, and beauty is fleeting, but a woman who fears the Lord is to be praised." This applies to both men and women—don't let physical attraction or charm be the deciding factor in who you date. Look for godly character, integrity, and a heart that loves and follows Jesus.

When we ignore God's purpose for dating, we invite complications, confusion, and heartache into our lives. But when we follow His plan—dating with intention, seeking spiritual compatibility, and asking the deep questions—we avoid the unnecessary pain that comes from doing things our own way.

God's plan for your love life is bigger and better than anything the world offers. Trust Him, follow His guidance, and date with purpose, not for fun.

TIME OF REFLECTION

Reflect on your dating experiences. Have you been dating with purpose, or have you been more focused on feelings and fun? Write down three intentional steps you can take to align your dating life with God's purpose. This might mean setting new boundaries, praying for wisdom, or asking deeper questions in your relationships.

Remember: God's plan for your relationships isn't just about momentary pleasure. It's about lasting joy and growing closer to Him. Don't settle for anything less than His best.

Chapter 4

I HATE HOW WE OVERLY INVEST IN DATING – THE DANGERS OF OVER-INVESTING IN RELATIONSHIPS

Let me be honest—over-investing in a relationship before it's time is dangerous. I've been there, and I learned the hard way. When we give too much of our hearts too soon, we set ourselves up for disappointment, hurt, and even sin. Many of us make the mistake of treating someone we're just dating like they're already our spouse. We pour in emotionally, spiritually, and even physically, only to be left broken and confused when things don't work out.

In this chapter, we're going to talk about why over-investing in relationships is a trap. We'll explore how giving too much of your heart can lead to physical compromise, including sexual sin. I'll share my story of how over-investing in relationships led me to become a single mom, and how I learned to do things differently when I met my husband. This chapter will also provide biblical principles for both men and women, reminding us to guard our hearts, set boundaries, and let God lead us as we date.

FAYE'S STORY: FROM OVER-INVESTING TO TRUSTING GOD

Before I met my husband, I made some serious mistakes in relationships. Like so many others, I thought that the more I gave, the more I'd be loved in return. I would over-invest in every way—emotionally, spiritually, and even physically. I'd find myself cooking, cleaning, and treating my boyfriends like they were already my husband. My heart would get attached too quickly, and where my heart went, my body followed. This over-investment led to compromises, and eventually, it led to sin.

I thought that giving more would secure the relationship, but it only made me vulnerable to heartache. I found myself caught up in sexual sin, and before I knew it, I became a single mom. The consequences of over-investing in relationships hit me hard, and I knew I had to change.

When I met my husband, I did things differently. I didn't give too much too soon. Instead, I was **watchful** and **prayerful**. I didn't treat him like a husband when we were just dating. I didn't feel the need to prove myself by doing all the cooking and cleaning. We took things slow, had fun, and let God guide our relationship. By not over-investing, I allowed God to lead us, and now we have a beautiful marriage and five wonderful children. This chapter is here to help you avoid the mistakes I made in the past.

WHY OVER-INVESTING LEADS TO EMOTIONAL AND PHYSICAL FORNICATION

When we give too much of our hearts in a relationship, we open the door to emotional and physical compromise. **Here's the truth:** When your heart goes, your body often follows. The Bible warns us to guard our hearts for a reason. Proverbs 4:23 says, "Above all else, guard your heart, for everything you do flows from it." Our emotions can drive our actions, and if we give too much of our hearts before a relationship is ready, we can end up in places we never intended to go—physically and spiritually.

Over-investing creates a false sense of intimacy and attachment that isn't backed by the commitment of marriage. It's like giving someone all of you when they haven't made the commitment to stand by you for life. This emotional attachment often leads to physical compromise, and in many cases, this leads to sexual sin. God's Word is clear about the importance of keeping ourselves pure before marriage. 1 Corinthians 6:18 tells us to "flee from sexual immorality." But when we over-invest emotionally, it becomes harder to flee because we've already allowed our hearts to be drawn in.

SPEAKING TO WOMEN: GUARD YOUR HEART AND TAKE IT EASY

Sis, I know how easy it is to fall into the trap of over-investing in a relationship. We want to feel loved, secure, and valued, so we give, give, and give. We cook, clean, and act like we're already married, thinking that if we do more, he'll love us more. But that's not how God designed relationships. God doesn't ask us to prove our worth by giving all of ourselves before marriage. He asks us to trust Him, to guard our hearts, and to let the man He has for us pursue us in the right way.

Here's the thing: when you over-invest emotionally and physically in a relationship, you're setting yourself up to be hurt. When we give too much emotionally, our hearts get tangled up in the relationship, and it becomes harder to keep our physical boundaries intact. This is why we must be careful. Proverbs 19:2 says, "Desire without knowledge is not good—how much more will hasty feet miss the way!" Take your time. There's no need to rush into giving everything of yourself to someone who hasn't committed to you in marriage.

You are not his wife until he's put a ring on it and made a covenant before God. Don't give someone husband-level access to your heart and life while you're still dating. It's okay to take things easy, have fun, and enjoy getting to know someone. Let him prove his intentions through his actions over time, not through what you do for him. Trust me, God's way is so much better than over-investing and ending up with a broken heart.

SPEAKING TO MEN:
GUARD YOUR HEART AND LEAD THE WAY

My brother, this message is for you too. As men, you are called to lead in relationships, and that includes leading with honor and respect. Ephesians 5:25 tells husbands to "love your wives, just as Christ loved the church and gave Himself up for her." While you're dating, you're preparing for marriage, and that means you should practice leading with love and purity now. Don't take advantage of a woman's desire to give. Just because she's offering to cook, clean, and do things for you doesn't mean you should let her. Instead, encourage her to guard her heart and set boundaries.

Furthermore, you must remember that she is not your wife yet. Do not take on husband duties prematurely. This will only cause confusion and possible heartbreak, especially if you chose to end the pursuit. Be careful and use wisdom in leading while dating.

Over-investing isn't just a problem for women—men can do it too. When you give too much of your resources, your heart and emotions too soon, you can find yourself compromising your standards and making decisions based on feelings instead of faith. Remember, you are called to lead with wisdom. Take your time, get to know her, and let God guide your relationship. Don't push for emotional or physical intimacy before it's time.

If you're truly interested in her, show her by your actions. Protect her heart, don't manipulate her into giving more of herself than she should. As a man, you have the responsibility to honor her and God by leading the relationship in purity and patience.

THE BIBLICAL PRINCIPLES FOR GUARDING YOUR HEART AND NOT OVER-INVESTING

God gives us principles in His Word that protect us from the pain of over-investing and compromise. Here are a few key biblical principles to keep in mind:

1. **Guard Your Heart (Proverbs 4:23)** Your heart is the wellspring of your life. Don't give it away too quickly. It's important to take time in relationships and not pour all your emotions into someone who hasn't committed to you. Your heart is valuable, and God wants you to protect it until the right time.

2. **Don't Awaken Love Before Its Time (Song of Solomon 2:7)** The Bible tells us not to "awaken love until it so desires." This means that there is a right time for love, and that time is in the context of marriage. Don't stir up romantic or physical feelings prematurely. Wait until the relationship is ready for that kind of intimacy—within the covenant of marriage.

3. **Flee from Sexual Immorality (1 Corinthians 6:18)** The Bible is clear: sexual intimacy is reserved for marriage. When we give too much of our hearts emotionally, it becomes easy to slip into physical fornication. Guard your body by guarding your heart. Don't over-invest physically, and keep your boundaries firm.

4. **Let God Lead (Proverbs 3:5-6)** Trust in the Lord with all your heart and lean not on your own understanding. In all your ways submit to Him, and He will make your paths straight. Let God lead your relationship, and don't rely on your feelings or emotions. If you trust Him, He will guide you toward the right person in the right way.

LESS IS MORE — TAKE IT EASY AND HAVE FUN

Over-investing in relationships causes more harm than good. When we give too much too soon, we open the door to emotional confusion, spiritual compromise, and even physical sin. **The truth is, less is more.** It's okay to take things easy, have fun, and let the relationship grow naturally. There's no need to rush or prove yourself by doing too much too soon.

When I met my husband, I didn't over-invest, and that made all the difference. I watched, prayed, and allowed the relationship to unfold in God's timing. Now, I'm living in the beauty of a God-honoring marriage with five wonderful children. God's way is better—take it slow, guard your heart, and trust Him.

TIME OF REFLECTION

Ask yourself if you've been over-investing in your relationships. Are you giving too much, emotionally or physically, for the stage of your relationship? Write down three things you can do to guard your heart more intentionally. Pray about your current or future relationships. Ask God to help you set boundaries and trust His timing.

Remember, your heart is precious—don't give it away too soon. Trust God's plan, and let Him guide your love story.

Chapter 5

I HATE THAT SO MANY BOUNDARIES HAVE BEEN BLURRED AND CROSSED

One of the biggest problems we face in dating today is the blurring of boundaries, especially when it comes to physical intimacy. The world tells us it's okay to go as far as we want in a relationship, but the Bible is clear: we must guard our bodies and hearts and live in purity. When we start crossing boundaries, emotional and physical lines get blurred, leading to sin and heartache. In this chapter, we're going to talk about how **too much time, too much talk, and too much touch can** lead to emotional fornication, which ultimately leads to physical fornication.

Let's get into the nitty-gritty of physical intimacy. It's a hot topic, and trust me, it can make or break a relationship. If you're not careful, you'll find yourself tangled up in feelings and situations that leave you feeling more confused than a cat at a dog show. So, whether you're a woman or a man, it's time to talk about how to navigate the physical side of dating without losing your mind—or your heart.

LADIES, LISTEN UP: SETTING THE STANDARD

Hey, queens! Let's have a heart-to-heart. You are the prize, and you need to start treating yourself like one! The world might tell you that you need to put out to keep a man interested, but that's a straight-up lie. Proverbs 31:10 says, "A wife of noble character who can find? She is worth far more than rubies." If he doesn't recognize your worth, then he ain't ready for the real you!

When it comes to physical intimacy, you've got to set the tone early. That means no jumping into bed just because he's cute and says all the right things. You deserve someone who respects your boundaries and is willing to wait. Don't let those butterflies trick you into rushing into something you might regret later.

EMOTIONAL AND PHYSICAL BOUNDARIES

Here's the deal: when you blur the lines between emotional and physical intimacy, you're setting yourself up for heartache. 1 Corinthians 6:18 warns us, "Flee from sexual immorality." Flee, girl! Don't walk, don't run—just get outta there! It's easier to avoid temptation than to try to resist it once you're knee-deep in feelings.

Set clear boundaries that align with your values and your relationship with God. Make sure he knows that you're not about that fast life. Your body is a temple (1 Corinthians 6:19), and it deserves to be treated with respect. If he's not willing to honor that, it's time to wave goodbye and keep it moving.

FOR THE MEN OF GOD: RESPECT AND RESPONSIBILITY

Alright, gentlemen, this is for you. Listen up! Physical intimacy isn't just about getting yours; it's about mutual respect and responsibility. If you're trying to build something real, you've got to be willing to invest in her emotionally as well. Ephesians 5:25 says, "Husbands, love your wives, just as Christ loved the church and gave himself up for her." This applies even in dating! If you're not ready to show that kind of love, you're not ready for the responsibility that comes with physical intimacy.

Understand that physical intimacy has power. It can either strengthen your bond or lead to confusion and heartache. Be clear about your intentions. If you're just looking for a good time, keep it real with her. Don't play with her heart just because you think she's fine. Women can sense when you're not being genuine, and trust me, she won't stick around for long if she feels used.

ESTABLISHING MUTUAL BOUNDARIES

For both ladies and gents, establishing mutual boundaries is key. Talk about your comfort levels and what you're both willing to share physically. Set clear expectations about where you stand and what you want.

1. **Communicate Openly:** Don't be afraid to have those awkward conversations. Discuss your values, your intentions, and your limits. Open communication builds trust and clarity, which are essential for a healthy relationship.

2. **Honor Each Other's Boundaries:** Respect goes both ways. If she's made it clear that she wants to wait, don't pressure her or try to change her mind. And ladies, if he's not comfortable going further than you'd like, respect that too.

3. **Find Activities That Strengthen the Connection:** Instead of jumping into bed, focus on activities that deepen your emotional bond. Go for a walk, have a deep conversation, or volunteer together. These moments can build intimacy without compromising your values.

UNDERSTANDING THE RISKS OF PHYSICAL INTIMACY

Let's break it down. Engaging in physical intimacy without a solid foundation can lead to emotional fallout, confusion, STD's, Babies and heartache. You don't want to be in a situation where you're questioning your worth because things didn't go as planned, or at worst end up like me in a homeless shelter as a new mom without the slightest clue of what to do next.

For ladies, physical intimacy can cloud your judgment. You might find yourself emotionally attached to someone who isn't meant for you, making it harder to walk away when you realize it's not working out. As women, we often invest our emotions into physical relationships, and that can lead to heartbreak when it doesn't turn out as expected.

For the fellas, remember that physical intimacy comes with a responsibility to protect her heart. If you're not ready for a relationship and/or a family, don't lead her on. Understand that every action has consequences, and breaking someone's heart can have a ripple effect that goes way beyond just the two of you. STOP PLAYING WITH FOLKS!

GOD'S GUIDANCE IN NAVIGATING INTIMACY

When in doubt, turn to the Word. God's principles are there to guide you in your dating life. Keep these scriptures in mind:

- **1 Thessalonians 4:3-5:** "It is God's will that you should be sanctified: that you should avoid sexual immorality; that each of you should learn to control your own body in a way that is holy and honorable, not in passionate lust like the pagans, who do not know God." This is a powerful reminder to keep your standards high and your desires in check.
- **Colossians 3:2:** "Set your minds on things that are above, not on things that are on earth." Focus on what truly matters, and don't let temporary feelings lead you away from God's best.

WALKING IN PURITY AND PURPOSE

As you navigate the dating scene, remember that physical intimacy should never overshadow your relationship with God or your values. Whether you're a woman or a man, setting boundaries is vital for building a healthy, loving relationship. By honoring yourself and your partner, you create a foundation built on trust, respect, and faith.

I do not care how good the sex is, you must repent and stop living in sin right now. A lit sex life isn't worth the fires of hell. Don't allow a moment of passion to lead to an eternity of regret.

Keep everything rooted in God's truth. A lifestyle of holiness never goes out of style, no matter what generation you're apart of. When you walk in purity and purpose, you'll attract the kind of love that honors both you and God. You deserve nothing less than the best!

HOLINESS IN DATING: A CALL TO RIGHTEOUSNESS

In today's dating landscape, the call to holiness is more crucial than ever. As believers, we are not only called to embrace a lifestyle that reflects Christ's love but also to resist the temptations that society throws our way. With sexual immorality becoming normalized, it's vital for Christians to stand firm in their faith and uphold biblical principles in their relationships.

In dating while walking in Holiness, you must watch those three T's. You may be asking yourself, What in the world is Faye talking about? I am so glad you asked. This is exactly what I mean. Too much TIME, too much TALK, too much TOUCH WILL LEAD TO EMOTIONAL Fornication, ultimately putting you at risk of sexual immorality and a lifestyle of disobedience to the King. If you give the enemy an inch, he will take at least a mile. Stop flirting with the fire of lust.

THE BIBLICAL FOUNDATION FOR HOLINESS

Scripture provides a clear framework for understanding our bodies and relationships in the light of God's design. **Hebrews 13:4** instructs us: "Let marriage be held in honor among all, and let the marriage bed be undefiled, for God will judge the sexually immoral and adulterous." This highlights the sanctity of marriage and the serious consequences of sexual sin. The emphasis is not just on the act itself but on the honor and respect we are to give to the institution of marriage.

1 Corinthians 6:18-20 further warns us: "Flee from sexual immorality. Every other sin a person commits is outside the body, but the sexually immoral person sins against his own body. Or do you not know that your body is a temple of the Holy Spirit within you, whom you have from God? You are not your own, for you were bought with a price. So glorify God in your body." This passage urges us to view our bodies as sacred, a dwelling place for the Holy Spirit, and to conduct ourselves in ways that honor God.

FOR WOMEN: EMBRACING HOLINESS

Ladies, the world may push you to conform, but your identity and worth are rooted in Christ.

- **Rejecting Cultural Norms:** The culture might tell you that it's acceptable to engage in casual relationships or premarital sex, especially if you feel lonely or pressured. However, **Romans 12:2** calls us to "not be conformed to this world, but be transformed by the renewal of your mind." Your decisions should be guided by God's truth, not societal pressures.

- **Understanding Your Worth:** Remember, you are a daughter of the King. **Psalm 139:14** reminds us, "I praise you, for I am fearfully and wonderfully made." When you know your worth, you'll be less likely to compromise in dating.

Steps to Repentance:

1. **Acknowledge Your Sin:** Take a moment to reflect on your choices and acknowledge areas where you have strayed from God's path.

2. **Seek Forgiveness:** Approach God with a sincere heart. He is always ready to forgive and restore you.

3. **End Toxic Relationships:** If you find yourself in a relationship that leads you away from God, it may be time to reassess its impact on your life.

Prayer of Repentance:

"Dear Heavenly Father, I come before You with a heavy heart, recognizing my failures in honoring You through my relationships. I ask for Your forgiveness for engaging in sexual sin. Cleanse my heart and guide my decisions as I strive to live a life that reflects Your holiness. Thank You for Your grace and love. In Jesus' name, Amen."

FOR MEN: A CALL TO RIGHTEOUS LEADERSHIP

Men, you have a critical role in fostering an atmosphere of holiness. Your leadership is essential, not just for your own purity but for those around you.

- **Lead with Integrity:** Ephesians 5:3 instructs, "But sexual immorality and all impurity or covetousness must not even be named among you, as is proper among saints." Your actions set the tone for how relationships unfold.

- **Accountability Matters:** Surround yourself with other men of God who will challenge you to uphold your values. **Proverbs 27:17** reminds us, "Iron sharpens iron, and one man sharpens another." Engage in accountability groups or mentorship that encourages a godly lifestyle.

Steps to Repentance:

1. **Reflect on Your Actions:** Consider how your behavior affects not just your life but the lives of others, particularly those you date.

2. **Seek God's Guidance:** Spend intentional time in prayer and study, asking God to reveal areas of your life that need transformation.

3. **Remove Temptations:** Be proactive in identifying situations or relationships that lead you toward sin, and take the necessary steps to avoid them.

Prayer of Repentance:

"Lord, I come to You today, acknowledging that I have fallen short of Your standards. I repent for my choices and ask for Your strength to walk in purity and integrity. Help me to lead well in my relationships and to honor You in everything I do. Thank You for Your forgiveness and for giving me another chance to live for You. In Jesus' name, Amen."

THE PATH TO HOLINESS

Choosing holiness in dating requires courage and commitment. It's not merely about following rules; it's about embracing a lifestyle that reflects Christ's love and righteousness.

- **Embrace Your Identity:** Understand that living a life of holiness is a testament to your faith. When you choose to honor God in your dating life, you are making a statement about who you are and whose you are.

- **Encourage Each Other:** Whether you're single, dating, or engaged, support each other in maintaining standards of purity. Share your struggles and victories with trusted friends or mentors who share your values.

- **Stay Grounded in Scripture:** Regularly meditate on God's Word to strengthen your resolve. Let the truths of the Bible inform your decisions and help you navigate the challenges of dating.

Ultimately, remember that it's never too late to turn back to Jesus. If you've strayed from His path, take heart—He is ready to welcome you back with open arms. Together, let's pursue holiness and strive to live lives that glorify God in all we do. By doing so, we not only protect ourselves but also honor the sanctity of the relationships we engage in, leading to a future that reflects His love and purpose.

THE PLACE OF NO RETURN: GUARDING AGAINST TEMPTATION

Let's get real about a critical issue in dating: the place of no return. This is that moment when too much touching and kissing has happened, and suddenly, fornication is knocking at the door. Many people point fingers at men, but I firmly believe that women have a significant role in guarding against premarital sex. Men, being physical creatures, can only resist for so long before temptation becomes overwhelming. Let's break this down for both men and women, supported by Scripture.

FOR WOMEN: THE CALL TO GUARD YOUR HEART

Ladies, it's time to take responsibility for your own boundaries. Proverbs 4:23 reminds us, "Above all else, guard your heart, for everything you do flows from it." This isn't just a cute saying; it's a call to action. You have the power to set the tone in your relationships. If you allow physical intimacy to escalate, you're not just inviting temptation; you're also risking your emotional health and spiritual well-being.

The Power of Touch:

Let's talk about the dangers of physical intimacy. Kissing may seem harmless, but it's a gateway to deeper connections. I believe that kissing leads to babies honey! Remember Song of Solomon 2:7: "Do not stir up or awaken love until it pleases." This verse isn't just a suggestion; it's a reminder that you have the authority to control the flow of intimacy.

When you allow kissing and excessive touching, you're stepping into dangerous territory. I am also 100% sure your hands are somewhere they should NOT be also! The tongue has immense power (Proverbs 18:21), and once you cross that line, it becomes increasingly challenging to return. You must practice modesty—not just in attire but in how you engage with your partner. By being intentional about your boundaries, you protect both your heart and your future.

How to Navigate This:

1. **Set Firm Boundaries:** Before getting involved, discuss what physical boundaries you're both comfortable with. Make it clear that certain behaviors are off-limits.

2. **Practice Modesty:** Modesty isn't just about how you dress; it's about how you present yourself in a relationship. Show respect for yourself and your values, which will help others do the same.

3. **Be Aware of the Place of No Return:** Recognize when things are getting too intimate. If you find yourself at that place of no return, it's time to step back and reassess the relationship.

FOR MEN: THE CALL TO LEAD WITH INTEGRITY

Now, let's talk to the men. As a man, you're called to lead in your relationships, but that leadership comes with great responsibility. Ephesians 5:25 commands, "Husbands, love your wives, as Christ loved the church and gave himself up for her." Even in dating, you should embody this sacrificial love.

The Responsibility to Flee:

Men, the reality is that you're physical creatures. But instead of giving in to temptation, you must actively flee from it. 1 Corinthians 6:18 states, "Flee from sexual immorality." This means to RUN! Many times you are sitting around enjoying the lustful situation and seeing how close you can get without penetration. STOP THIS NOW MAN OF GOD! As the lead you must man up and lead. Sometimes leadership looks like getting your stuff, getting in your car and leaving IMMEDIATELY! SO let's not continue to wait until the heat of the moment; take proactive steps to avoid compromising situations.

How to Navigate This:

- **Lead by Example:** If you're serious about honoring God in your relationship, show that by setting the right tone. Respect the boundaries set by your partner and encourage her to uphold her standards.

- **Be Mindful of Your Actions:** Understand that physical intimacy can escalate quickly. Keep your hands and lips in check. Remember, "A man without self-control is like a city broken into and left without walls" (Proverbs 25:28).

- **Encourage Modesty:** Support your partner in her journey to practice modesty. When both partners are committed to setting boundaries, it creates a healthier environment for your relationship.

THE POWER OF TEAMWORK

Ultimately, both men and women must work together to avoid the place of no return. It's not just one person's job; it's a joint effort to honor God and respect each other's boundaries. By being mindful of your actions, practicing modesty, and communicating openly, you can create a relationship that thrives on mutual respect and faith.

Remember, as Christians, we're called to be blameless in our actions. By taking these principles to heart, you can navigate the dating scene in a way that honors God, protects your heart, and fosters a loving relationship that can withstand the tests of time. Let's strive to guard our hearts and live out our faith, keeping temptation at bay and honoring the sanctity of our bodies and relationships!

THE DANGERS OF SPIRITUAL INTIMACY IN DATING

Let's dive into a vital yet often overlooked topic in the realm of dating: spiritual intimacy. While sharing your faith and spiritual experiences can be enriching, too much spiritual intimacy with someone you're dating can lead to significant pitfalls. This is especially true when it creates a false sense of growth and connection that may not align with God's intentions for your life. Let's explore this concept for both women and men, anchored in Scripture and biblical principles.

FOR WOMEN: THE IMPORTANCE OF DISCERNMENT

Ladies, it's crucial to understand the weight of spiritual intimacy. 1 Corinthians 6:17 tells us, "But he who is joined to the Lord becomes one spirit with him." This oneness is a profound connection meant for marriage, not casual dating. Sharing deep spiritual experiences, like prayer or worship, too soon in a relationship can create a strong bond. It will be hard to break.

The Dangers of Oversharing:

When you open up your heart and spirit to someone you're dating, it can lead to a false sense of closeness. This strong bond can blur the lines between friendship and love. You may find yourself believing that you're growing spiritually together, but it might just be an illusion. Intimacy—spiritual, emotional, or physical— is for a committed, ideally, married, relationship.

How to Navigate This:

1. **Establish Boundaries:** Set clear boundaries around your spiritual practices. While it's essential to share your faith, be mindful of how deeply you share early on in the relationship.

2. **Encourage Group Worship:** Instead of one-on-one spiritual activities, consider engaging in group worship or

community events. This keeps the focus on your faith while maintaining appropriate boundaries.

3. **Seek God's Guidance:** Always pray for discernment. Ask God to reveal whether this person is meant to be a part of your spiritual journey, or if it's time to step back.

FOR MEN: LEADING WITH WISDOM

Gentlemen, as you pursue relationships, recognize the responsibility you have in cultivating spiritual intimacy. Ephesians 5:23 reminds us that "the husband is the head of the wife even as Christ is the head of the church." This leadership should begin early in the dating process, emphasizing integrity and wisdom.

The Risk of False Intimacy:

When you rush into spiritual intimacy, you risk creating a bond that may lead to emotional and physical intimacy as well. It's easy to confuse spiritual closeness with romantic interest, but this can set the stage for confusion and disappointment.

How to Navigate This:

- **Lead with Clarity:** Be transparent about your intentions. If you're serious about pursuing a relationship, communicate your desire to grow together, but be cautious about how deep that spiritual connection goes too soon.

- **Establish Accountability:** Encourage accountability between you and your partner. Discuss how you can both maintain boundaries in your spiritual growth while still supporting each other.

- **Avoid Misleading Connections:** Recognize that intense spiritual conversations and experiences can create a misleading sense of readiness for marriage. It's crucial to assess whether your connection is truly grounded in God's will or just an emotional high.

THE BALANCE OF SPIRITUAL INTIMACY

Both men and women must approach spiritual intimacy with discernment. It's essential to share your faith but to do so in a way that honors God and respects the sanctity of your relationship.

Proverbs 3:5-6 encourages us to "Trust in the Lord with all your heart, and do not lean on your own understanding. In all your ways acknowledge him, and he will make straight your paths." As you date, let these verses guide your choices. They should align with God's purpose for your life.

Remember, spiritual intimacy is a profound bond meant for marriage. Be aware of the dangers and use discernment. Doing so can help you build a relationship that honors God and enriches your spiritual journey. It will also prepare you for a loving, committed partnership in the future. Let's strive to maintain the sanctity of spiritual intimacy and seek God's guidance in all our relationships!

Chapter 6

I HATE THAT SO MANY PEOPLE ARE FAKE CHRISTIANS

In today's world, many people claim to be Christians, but their lives tell a different story. They may say they follow Jesus, but their actions show otherwise. This becomes especially dangerous when we are dating, because it's easy to fall for someone's words without looking closely at their actions. We need to recognize that not everyone who says "I'm a Christian" is truly following Christ. Some people are simply **pretending** to be Christians, and if we're not careful, we can get caught up in relationships that pull us away from God.

This chapter focuses on recognizing **false believers**—people who claim to follow Jesus but live in ways that lead us into sin. It's about how engaging in sexual behavior, like sending nude photos or engaging in inappropriate conversations, is a sign of spiritual danger. We'll also discuss the importance of **not dating to convert someone** and how that can be a trap that leads to heartbreak and spiritual compromise. If you find yourself in this situation, it's time to repent and turn back to true faith in Christ.

We'll explore biblical warnings about wolves in sheep's clothing, the dangers of causing someone to stumble, and how to cut off anything in your life that leads to sin. If you are pretending to be a Christian or if you're dating someone who is, this chapter is for you. The time to repent is now.

THE DANGERS OF PRETENDING TO FOLLOW CHRIST

One of the most dangerous things you can encounter in dating is someone who **pretends to follow Christ** but doesn't live it out. Jesus warned us about this in Matthew 7:15-16 when He said, "Watch out for false prophets. They come to you in sheep's clothing, but inwardly they are ferocious wolves. By their fruit, you will recognize them."

False believers can appear harmless and even charming, but if their lives don't show the fruit of a real relationship with Jesus, they are wolves in disguise. These people might say all the right things—they may go to church, talk about God, and act like a believer—but their actions reveal their true character. Their hearts aren't transformed by Christ, and they lead others into temptation and sin. This is why you must learn to check the fruit in your partner or your potential partner's life. Become a fruit inspector!

When we date someone who isn't truly following Jesus, we open ourselves up to **compromise**. They might encourage us to cross boundaries, pressure us into physical intimacy, or push us to do things that don't align with God's will. They may even ask for inappropriate things, like **nude photos** or sexual messages. Sisters and brothers, this is not what kingdom Christ centered love looks like. If someone is asking you to engage in these kinds of behaviors, **they are not leading you to Jesus**—they are leading you into sin.

STOP LEADING OTHERS INTO SIN

One of the clearest signs of a false believer is someone who **causes others to stumble.** If the person you're dating is leading you into temptation—whether through sexual pressure, inappropriate conversations, or asking for things like nude photos—they are pulling you away from God's plan for your life. You need to run! Jesus was very clear about how serious this is. In Matthew 18:6, He said, "If anyone causes one of these little ones—those who believe in Me—to stumble, it would be better for them to have a large millstone hung around their neck and to be drowned in the depths of the sea."

This is strong language from Jesus, but it shows us how seriously God views leading others into sin. If you are in a relationship where someone is pressuring you to sin—whether it's sexual sin or anything else—you need to recognize that this person is not following Christ. A true believer would help you **flee from sin**, not lead you into it.

1 Corinthians 6:18 tells us to "Flee from sexual immorality. All other sins a person commits are outside the body, but whoever sins sexually, sins against their own body." God intended sex to

be a beautiful expression of love within the covenant of marriage. Anything outside of that is sexual immorality, and we must run from it.

If you're in a relationship where you or the other person is crossing physical boundaries, sending inappropriate messages, or engaging in behaviors that dishonor God, **you are in danger**. You're not leading each other to Jesus—you're leading each other to sin. It's time to stop and turn back to holiness. Repent.

DON'T DATE TO CONVERT: THE TRAP OF UNEQUALLY YOKED RELATIONSHIPS

One of the biggest mistakes Christians make in dating is thinking they can **date someone to convert them**. Maybe you meet someone who isn't a Christian, but you think, "If I date them, I can bring them to church, and they'll change." This is a dangerous trap. The Bible has warned us about being unequally yoked in relationships.

2 Corinthians 6:14 says, "Do not be yoked together with unbelievers. For what do righteousness and wickedness have in common? Or what fellowship can light have with darkness?" When we date someone who doesn't share our faith, we are tying ourselves to someone who is pulling in the opposite direction. They may not understand or value the things of God, and this can lead to serious spiritual problems.

Here's the truth: **You cannot date someone into the Kingdom of God**. Only Jesus can change someone's heart, and it's not your job to "fix" them. If you're dating someone who isn't committed to following Jesus, it will lead to compromise. You might find yourself lowering your standards, giving in to pressure, or even questioning your own faith because the person you're with isn't on the same page spiritually.

I've seen many women and men fall into this trap, thinking they can bring their partner closer to God through dating. Dating is NOT an evangelism tool. What often happens is the opposite: the Christian ends up being pulled away from God. It's important to **trust God to bring you a partner** who is already committed to following Jesus. Don't date to convert—date someone who's already running after Jesus, and run together toward Him.

SPEAKING TO WOMEN: BE WATCHFUL AND PROTECT YOUR HEART

Sis, it's easy to fall for someone's words, especially if they seem to know how to talk about God. But watch their actions. Are they leading you closer to Jesus, or are they leading you into sin? If they're asking you for nude photos, pressuring you to be physical, or encouraging behaviors that don't line up with God's Word, they are not following Jesus, no matter what they say.

Your body is a temple of the Holy Spirit (1 Corinthians 6:19-20). It's precious, and it belongs to God. Don't give parts of yourself—emotionally, spiritually, or physically—to someone who doesn't honor your boundaries or your faith. If you're with someone who is causing you to stumble, it's time to step back and protect your heart. True love waits for marriage, and a man who truly loves and follows God will honor your purity, not pressure you into compromise.

God has called us to be women of purity and holiness, not to lead others into sin. Proverbs 7 warns of the dangers of a seductive woman, and we must be careful not to use our words, appearance, or actions to draw men into temptation. If you're dressing or behaving in ways that invite lust, or if you're encouraging physical boundaries to be crossed, you're leading that man into sin—and that dishonors both him and God. Instead, honor God with your body and your actions, and help the men around you walk in purity. True beauty and love are found in holiness, not seduction.

SPEAKING TO MEN: LEAD WITH PURITY, NOT LUST

Bro, if you're leading a woman into sin—whether it's through physical pressure, asking for inappropriate photos, or encouraging sexual conversations—you are not honoring her or God. You need to be delivered! You are called to lead with purity, not lust. Ephesians 5:3 says, "But among you there must not be even a hint of sexual immorality, or of any kind of impurity... because these are improper for God's holy people."

Don't be the reason a woman stumbles in her faith. If you're claiming to follow Christ, your actions need to reflect that. If you find yourself leading someone into temptation, it's time to repent. Stop sending sexual messages. Stop pushing physical boundaries. And stop pretending to be a Christian if your life doesn't show it. A true man of God will lead a woman toward holiness, not toward his bed. He will also not allow a woman to seduce him into her bed as well! You must in these times fight for your walk with Jesus. It will not be easy but through the power of the Holy Spirit you can overcome lust and walk in Holiness.

God calls you to lead with strength and purity, not to be led into temptation. Proverbs 6:25 warns, "Do not lust in your heart after her beauty or let her captivate you with her eyes." If a woman is trying to seduce you through her words, appearance, or actions, remember that giving in to sexual sin dishonors both you and God. You are responsible for guarding your heart and fleeing from temptation (1 Corinthians 6:18). Don't allow your desires to overtake your commitment to holiness. Stand firm, protect your purity, and honor God in how you lead your relationships.

CUT OFF WHAT CAUSES YOU TO STUMBLE

As believers, we are responsible for cutting off anything in our lives that causes us to stumble into sin. Jesus said in Matthew 5:29-30, "If your right eye causes you to stumble, gouge it out and throw it away. It is better for you to lose one part of your body than for your whole body to be thrown into hell. And if your right hand causes you to stumble, cut it off and throw it away. It is better for you to lose one part of your body than for your whole body to go into hell."

Jesus wasn't telling us to literally harm ourselves. He was saying that sin is so serious that we need to **radically remove anything** from our lives that causes us to fall into temptation. This might mean cutting off a relationship that's leading you into sin, deleting contacts or apps that encourage inappropriate behavior, or setting stricter boundaries to protect your purity.

True followers of Christ understand that holiness is non-negotiable. God calls us to be holy because He is holy (1 Peter 1:16). That means we don't play with sin, we don't compromise our standards, and we don't let anyone pull us away from God's will for our lives.

REFLECTION: ARE YOU TRULY FOLLOWING CHRIST?

Take a moment to reflect on your current relationship or dating life. Ask yourself these questions:

- Are you pretending to follow Christ while living in sin?
- Is the person you're dating leading you closer to God, or are they causing you to stumble?
- Have you crossed physical or emotional boundaries that dishonor God?
- Are you dating someone in the hope of converting them, even though they don't truly follow Jesus?
- What steps can you take to cut off anything that is causing you to stumble into sin?

If any of these questions reveal areas of compromise, now is the time to repent and return to God.

A CALL TO REPENTANCE: TURN BACK TO GOD

If you've been pretending to follow Christ, it's time to repent. Stop living in sexual sin and leading others into temptation. The Bible warns us that those who live in habitual sin will not inherit the kingdom of God (Galatians 5:19-21). But there is grace, forgiveness, and healing available if you turn back to Him now.

PRAYER OF SALVATION

Lord Jesus, I come to You today, realizing that I have been pretending to follow You, but my heart has not truly been Yours. I confess my sins and ask for Your forgiveness. I believe that You died on the cross for my sins and rose again to give me new life. Today, I surrender my life to You completely. I turn away from my sin, and I invite You to be my Lord and Savior. Help me to follow You for real, with all my heart, from this day forward. Thank You for Your grace, mercy, and love. In Jesus' name, Amen.

PRAYER FOR REPENTANCE

Let's come before God in repentance:

PRAYER FOR WOMEN

Father, I come before You with a humble heart, knowing that I have crossed boundaries and allowed sin into my life. I repent of any behavior that dishonors You and ask for Your forgiveness. Help me to set boundaries that protect my heart, mind, and body. Guide me in choosing relationships that honor You, and give me the strength to walk in purity. In Jesus' name, Amen.

PRAYER FOR MEN

Lord, I confess that I have led others into temptation and have allowed lust and impurity to rule my actions. I repent of my sins and ask You to cleanse me from all unrighteousness. Help me to lead with purity, to protect the women in my life, and to walk in a way that reflects Your holiness. Give me the strength to flee from temptation and to live as a true follower of Christ. In Jesus' name, Amen.

Chapter 7

I HATE CHRISTIAN DATING BECAUSE OF THE PRESSURES OF PURITY CULTURE

We've all heard the message growing up in church: "Stay pure until marriage." The idea of purity is drilled into us from a young age, and while this is an **important biblical truth**, there's a part of this message that can create an identity crisis. **Purity culture** sometimes can make you feel like your worth is tied to whether or not we've stayed a virgin. It can leave us thinking, "If I've messed up, I'm broken or unworthy." But here's the truth: **your identity is not in your virginity**.

Let me be real with you. We know plenty of people who are virgins, but they're stuck in the cycle of **watching porn** or **masturbating**. They might have stayed away from physical sex, but their minds and hearts are not living in purity. But, we've seen former fornicators and ex-prostitutes transformed by the Power of God. These people now walk in holiness. It's due to what Jesus Christ has done for them, not their own actions.

The Holy Spirit has renewed, restored, and empowered them to live lives that honor God.

This is why it's so important to understand that **your identity is not in your virginity**—it's in Christ alone. Whether you've stayed a virgin or made mistakes in the past, God's love for you is the same and Jesus Christ shed his blood for both the virgin and the non virgin. Purity isn't just about staying away from sex before marriage. It's about letting the **Holy Spirit** transform your heart, mind, and life so that you live fully for God. The only way to walk in true purity is by relying on God's power, not our own strength.

THE PRESSURE OF PURITY CULTURE

In the Christian world, there's often a huge emphasis on staying **sexually pure** before marriage. And this is good because it aligns with biblical teaching. God's Word tells us to avoid sexual immorality and keep ourselves pure. **1 Thessalonians 4:3-4** says, "It is God's will that you should be sanctified: that you should avoid sexual immorality; that each of you should learn to control your own body in a way that is holy and honorable."

But sometimes the way this message is presented creates a heavy weight of pressure. Purity culture often idolizes virginity. It makes it seem like the most important thing to hold onto. The problem with this is that it can make people feel like their **worth** is tied to their sexual history.

If you've made mistakes, you might feel like you're damaged goods, like your value is somehow less. This is a **lie from the enemy. God doesn't see you as broken** because of your past. When you come to Him with a repentant heart, He forgives and restores you. **Isaiah 1:18** tells us, "Though your sins are like scarlet, they shall be as white as snow; though they are red as crimson, they shall be like wool." In Christ, you are made new.

At the same time, there are people who have held onto their virginity but still struggle with things like **pornography** or **masturbation**. Just because someone is physically a virgin doesn't mean they are living in purity. **Matthew 5:28** says, "But I tell you that anyone who looks at a woman lustfully has already committed adultery with her in his heart." Purity goes beyond physical actions; it's about the condition of your heart.

DON'T GET IT TWISTED!

Although **purity culture** can sometimes create unhealthy pressure, it's important to remember the powerful truth that **Jesus Christ is a Keeper**. He is fully able to help you maintain your virginity until marriage. And let me tell you, that is a beautiful thing! In a world that often dismisses the value of virginity, it's actually something to be celebrated. Virginity is a gift, and when you honor God with your body, **Jesus is proud** of your commitment to Him. 1 Corinthians 6:19-20 reminds us that we should honor God with our bodies, which are temples of the Holy Spirit.

We often think the only powerful testimonies are rescue stories from deep sin. But don't miss this: the **most beautiful**

testimony can be the one where **Jesus kept you from sin** in the first place. It's a story of God's grace and strength that allows you to walk in purity from the beginning. **Jude 1:24** says, "To Him who is able to keep you from stumbling and to present you before His glorious presence without fault and with great joy." Jesus is fully capable of keeping you from stumbling, and He delights in your obedience.

You don't have to go through all the heartache and baggage that comes from sin in order to experience God's grace and love. Jesus is able to help you avoid those painful detours and keep you walking in His light. Take my husband, for instance. He was a virgin when we got married, and he waited on God's perfect timing. Because of his love for Jesus and his commitment to **biblical principles**, I was able to share in the blessing of his obedience. **Psalm 119:9** says, "How can a young person stay on the path of purity? By living according to Your word." My husband chose to live by God's Word, and because of that, we both received the blessing of his purity.

Obedience to God's Word doesn't just benefit you—it blesses your future spouse too. It's amazing what God can do when you trust Him to lead your life, even in areas like sexual purity. Don't feel like you have to have a story of redemption from sin to be valuable. Jesus honors and blesses those who trust Him to keep them from sin. **Philippians 1:6** reminds us that God, who began a good work in you, will carry it on to completion. When you let Jesus be your Keeper, He will guide you all the way to a marriage that honors Him!

YOUR IDENTITY IS IN CHRIST, NOT IN YOUR VIRGINITY OR LACK THEREOF

The biggest problem with **purity culture** is that it can make us believe our identity is wrapped up in whether or not we've stayed a virgin. But the truth is, **all of our worth is found in Christ alone.** Whether you've made mistakes or you've followed all the rules, your value doesn't come from what you've done. Your value comes from **who you are** in Christ.

2 Corinthians 5:17 says, "Therefore, if anyone is in Christ, the new creation has come: The old has gone, the new is here!" When you surrender your life to Jesus, you are a **new creation.** Your past doesn't define you anymore—God's grace does. We all need God's grace because none of us are perfect. Some of us may have stayed virgins but struggled with lust, while others may have fallen into sexual sin but have been restored by God's grace. Either way, our identity is in Christ, not our past.

We know people who were once trapped in lives of sexual sin—whether they were fornicators or even prostitutes—who have now been completely transformed by God's power. These men and women are walking in **true purity**, not because of their own efforts, but because of the **Holy Spirit** working in them. They are living proof that **God's grace can transform anyone**, no matter where they've been.

GOD'S STANDARD FOR PURITY: A MATTER OF THE HEART

God's call to purity isn't just about following a set of rules—it's about having a heart that's fully surrendered to Him. You can stay a virgin and still have an impure heart if your mind and desires are focused on lust. **Matthew 5:8** says, "Blessed are the pure in heart, for they will see God." True purity starts in the heart. It's about letting God transform your mind, your thoughts, and your desires so that everything you do is for His glory.

If you've made mistakes, don't let the enemy convince you that you're no longer valuable or that you can't live in purity. **God is a God of restoration**. He can redeem your past and give you a future filled with hope and purpose. **Joel 2:25** says, "I will restore to you the years that the locust hath eaten." Whatever has been lost or broken in your life, God can restore it.

Even if you've struggled with things like pornography or lustful thoughts, God can set you free from those chains. **Romans 12:2** tells us, "Do not conform to the pattern of this world, but be transformed by the renewing of your mind." God doesn't just want you to follow a list of rules—He wants to transform your entire life through the power of the Holy Spirit.

LIVING IN FREEDOM AND GRACE

Living in purity isn't something you do in your own strength—it's something you do through the power of the Holy Spirit. You don't have to rely on willpower alone to stay pure. God has given you everything you need to live a life that honors Him, and that includes walking in purity. **Galatians 5:16** says, "So I say, walk by the Spirit, and you will not gratify the desires of the flesh."

If you've fallen short, if you've made mistakes, there is **freedom in Christ**. You don't have to carry the weight of your past. God's grace is greater than any sin, and He offers you a fresh start today. **Lamentations 3:22-23** reminds us, "Because of the Lord's great love we are not consumed, for His compassions never fail. They are new every morning; great is Your faithfulness." Every day is a new opportunity to walk in the freedom and purity that God has for you.

At the end of the day, your identity is not found in your virginity or your past. **Your identity is in Christ alone.** Whether you've stayed pure or made mistakes, God's love for you never changes. He offers you grace, forgiveness, and a new beginning every day.

Don't let the pressures of purity culture make you feel like you have to be perfect to be loved by God. You are already loved, already chosen, and already redeemed because of what Jesus has done for you. Your identity, anchored in Him, unlocks true freedom. Embrace this assurance. Walk confidently, knowing your essence is divinely secured.

TIME OF REFLECTION

Take a moment to reflect on where you are. Ask yourself:

- Have I been feeling pressure to be perfect because of the purity culture?
- Do I believe that my worth is tied to my virginity or my past mistakes?

- Am I trusting in God's grace and relying on the Holy Spirit to help me live a life of purity?
- Have you felt like your testimony doesn't matter because it's not like everyone else? If so you need to repent, rejoice and start thanking God for Keeping You!!

If you've been carrying shame or pressure, now is the time to release it to God. He is ready to help you walk in freedom.

PRAYER FOR FREEDOM AND IDENTITY IN CHRIST

Lord, I come before You, asking for Your grace and strength. Help me to remember that my identity is in You alone and not in my past or my mistakes. Thank You for Your love, Your forgiveness, and Your power that enables me to walk in purity. I surrender my heart, my mind, and my body to You. Help me to live a life that honors You in every way. In Jesus' name, Amen.

Chapter 8

I HATE THAT WE DO NOT KNOW HOW TO HAVE REAL RELATIONSHIPS BECAUSE OF TRAUMA AND UNHEALED WOUNDS

Many of us are carrying around wounds we haven't healed from—wounds that come from past relationships, childhood trauma, betrayal, or hurtful experiences. These wounds, if not dealt with, show up in our relationships, causing us to create **trauma bonds**, emotional baggage, and toxic patterns. We enter relationships with the hope that they'll make us feel whole, but the truth is, **you cannot date yourself whole**. You can't find healing by adding another person into your life if you're still broken inside. You must go to the Lord, seek therapy, and allow God to heal you before you invite someone else into your heart.

In this chapter, we're going to talk about the importance of getting whole before you date. I'll share my personal story about how I had to spend years healing, learning how to forgive, and releasing the pain of my past before I could truly find love again. I had to stop running from my trauma and actually face it with God's help. And I want to encourage you that you can't keep running from your own pain—**hurt people hurt people**, and if you don't take the time to heal, you'll only bring more hurt into your relationships.

YOU CAN'T DATE YOURSELF WHOLE – HEALING COMES FROM GOD, NOT RELATIONSHIPS

One of the biggest lies we believe is that a relationship will fix everything. We mistakenly think that finding the right person will end our pain and trauma at times. But that's not true. **A relationship doesn't make you whole**—only God can do that. Colossians 2:10 reminds us that Christ has brought you to fullness." Your wholeness comes from your relationship with Jesus, not from dating.

When you try to date yourself into healing, you put unrealistic expectations on the other person. You expect them to fill the voids, heal the wounds, and fix what's broken in you. But the truth is, no human being can carry that weight. If you're not healed and whole in Christ, you'll bring those unhealed wounds into your relationship and end up hurting the other person, too.

Hurt people hurt people—that's a reality we need to face. When you don't deal with your own pain, you end up causing pain in your relationships. You might project your insecurity, fear, or anger onto your partner, expecting them to fix something that only God can heal. If you're not healthy enough to date, you need to take a step back and let God do the healing work in you first.

MY JOURNEY OF HEALING AND LEARNING TO FORGIVE

I know this first hand because I lived it. After going through heartbreak and becoming a single mom, I knew I wasn't ready to date again. My heart was still broken, and I was carrying so much pain from my past. I was what you would call a man hater. Anger was literally the only emotion I could feel and express. After lots of tears and guidance from my community I know I had to **stop running from my trauma** and actually face it with God's help. I spent years healing, going to therapy, and learning how to forgive. It wasn't easy, but it was necessary.

One of the hardest things I had to learn was how to **forgive**—not just in my mind, but from my heart. Matthew 5:44 says, "But I tell you, love your enemies and pray for those who persecute you." I had to pray for the people who hurt me, despitefully used me, and walked away. I had to bless the people who cursed me, and that was not easy. But in that process of releasing bitterness, I found freedom. I had to let go of everyone and everything that had ever wounded me. I am so thankful for my amazing spiritual parents Apostle Tony Wade and Prophetess Felecia Wade for teaching me these principles and walking with me through them.

You cannot move forward until you forgive and release the pain, offenses and betrayals of your past. The Bible says in

Ephesians 4:31-32, "Get rid of all bitterness, rage, and anger. Be kind and compassionate to one another. Forgive each other, just as in Christ God forgave you."" I had to forgive, not for their sake, but for mine. Holding onto bitterness and anger was only keeping me stuck in my trauma.

When I stopped running from my trauma and cried out to the Lord for help, got into therapy to face it head-on, God began to heal me. I went to therapy, talked through my issues, was even placed on medication for depression at one of lowest points, while continuously praying for God's help in my journey of healing. It took time—years, actually—but by the time I met my husband, I was whole in Christ. I wasn't looking for him to fix me, and I wasn't projecting my pain onto him. We were able to build a healthy, godly relationship because I had taken the time to heal first.

HURT PEOPLE HURT PEOPLE – WHY MANY AREN'T HEALTHY ENOUGH TO DATE

If you're not healed from your past, you're not ready to date. Point blank period. This might be a hard truth to hear, but it's necessary. Many people jump into relationships thinking that love will fix their issues, but it doesn't. If you're still carrying emotional baggage, unresolved trauma, or unforgiveness, those things will show up in your relationship, causing problems for both you and the person you're with.

Trauma bonds are formed when two people connect over shared pain or trauma, but instead of bringing healing, the relationship reinforces the hurt. You might find yourself attracted to someone because they've been through similar experiences, but this kind of bond is unhealthy. You're not building the relationship on love or godly values—you're building it on pain. That's not what God wants for you. Codependency is another harmful bond in a relationship as well.

God wants you to **heal and be whole** before you enter a relationship. He doesn't want you to be stuck in a cycle of toxic patterns, repeating the same mistakes over and over again. If you're not healthy enough to date, it's okay to take a step back. You don't need to rush into a relationship when your heart is still wounded. Trust that God will bring the right person into your life at the right time—when you're healed and ready to love from a place of wholeness.

STOP RUNNING FROM YOUR TRAUMA – SEEK HEALING NOW

It's easy to keep running from your trauma, to keep pushing it down and hoping that it will go away. But the truth is, your trauma won't disappear on its own. You have to confront it, face it, and seek healing. God is waiting to heal you, but you have to be willing to do the work.

Psalm 34:18 says, "The Lord is close to the brokenhearted and saves those who are crushed in spirit." God is near to you, even in your pain. He sees your wounds, and He wants to heal you, but you have to let Him. That might mean going to therapy, talking to a trusted counselor, or praying through your trauma. Healing is a journey, but it's one that you don't have to take alone.

Don't rush into a relationship thinking that it will heal you. Relationships don't heal brokenness—God does. Let Him make you whole, so that when you do enter a relationship, you're coming from a place of strength, not brokenness.

AVOID TRAUMA BOND DATING – SEEK GOD'S WHOLENESS FIRST

Trauma bonds are dangerous because they create a false sense of intimacy. When two people bond over their shared pain, they mistake that connection for love. But real love is not built on trauma—it's built on Christ. Trauma bonds often lead to codependency, emotional manipulation, and toxicity. You may feel "needed" in the relationship, but it's not a healthy kind of need. It's a bond that traps both people in their pain instead of leading them to healing.

If you find yourself in a relationship where the bond is based on trauma, it's time to reevaluate. Ask yourself if this relationship is helping you grow in Christ, or if it's just keeping you stuck in the same patterns. Real love is healing, freeing, and God-centered. It's not built on pain, but on peace.

Matthew 11:28-30 tells us to come to Jesus for rest and healing: "Come to me, all you who are weary and burdened, and I will give you rest. Take my yoke upon you and learn from me, for I am gentle and humble in heart, and you will find rest for your souls." If you're carrying the weight of trauma, Jesus is inviting you to lay it down at His feet. He will give you rest, healing, and wholeness.

SPEAKING TO WOMEN: TAKE THE TIME TO HEAL

Sis, if you've been carrying pain, heartbreak, or trauma from your past, it's time to let God heal you. Don't rush into a relationship just to feel better. Take the time to heal, to forgive, and to release the people who have hurt you. It's not fair to expect someone else to fix what's broken in you. Only God can do that.

I know it's hard, but healing is worth it. Let God make you whole so that when the right man comes into your life, you're ready to love him from a place of strength, not brokenness. Trust that God has a beautiful plan for your life, but that plan starts with healing.

Remember this: if you haven't allowed God to heal your heart, it will be difficult to follow and submit to the man He may send into your life. Unhealed wounds can create walls of distrust, fear, and insecurity, making it hard to open your heart fully. When you're not whole, you may struggle with control, jealousy, or pushing him away, even if he's the right man. True submission in love requires emotional and spiritual health, and that only comes when you've allowed God to heal your past hurts and make you whole.

SPEAKING TO MEN: BE WHOLE BEFORE YOU LEAD

Bro, if you're carrying emotional baggage or trauma, it's time to deal with it. Don't try to lead a relationship when you're not whole yourself. A man of God is called to lead with strength, and that means being emotionally healthy and spiritually grounded.

Take the time to seek healing, whether it's through prayer, therapy, or talking to a mentor. Don't let your unhealed wounds damage your future relationships. God has a purpose for your life, but you need to be whole in Christ before you can truly lead someone else in love.

Remember this: if you haven't allowed God to heal you, it will be difficult to lead the wife He may send you. Unhealed men often lead from a place of insecurity, which can result in hurt, control, and damage to the good things God wants to give them. Ephesians 5:25 calls men to love their wives as Christ loved the church—with sacrificial, selfless love. But without healing, you can't lead in the way God intended. A man must first allow God to restore and heal his heart so that he can lead with love, wisdom, and security, just as God commands.

BIBLICAL PRINCIPLES: WHOLENESS COMES FROM GOD

The Bible is clear that our wholeness comes from God alone, not from relationships. Jesus said in John 10:10, "I have come that they may have life, and have it to the full." He wants you to live a full, healed, and whole life. But that fullness comes from Him—not from a partner, not from dating, and not from anything else the world offers.

God is the source of your healing. He is the one who binds up your wounds and makes you whole. Before you enter a relationship, seek wholeness in Christ. Let Him heal your heart, so that you can love from a place of strength and health, not from brokenness.

HEALING FIRST, LOVE LATER

Before you can build a healthy relationship, you need to let God heal your heart. Stop running from your trauma, stop expecting others to fix you, and take the time to heal. God is the source of your wholeness, and when you seek Him first, He will prepare you for the love He has in store for you.

TIME OF REFLECTION

Take a moment to reflect on your emotional and spiritual health. Ask yourself:

- Am I carrying unhealed trauma or pain from my past?
- Have I been running from my trauma instead of seeking healing?
- Am I expecting someone else to fix what's broken in me, instead of letting God heal me?
- What steps can I take to seek healing and wholeness before I enter a relationship?

If you're carrying any unhealed wounds, now is the time to bring them to God. He is ready to heal you, but you have to let Him.

PRAYER FOR HEALING

Lord, I come to You with a broken heart. I've been carrying pain, trauma, and wounds that I can't heal on my own. I ask for Your healing power to work in me. Help me to forgive those who have hurt me and to release the pain I've been holding onto. Teach me how to seek healing in You, and give me the strength to walk in wholeness before I seek love in a relationship. I trust that You will make me whole and prepare me for the right relationship in Your perfect timing. In Jesus' name, Amen.

Chapter 9

I HATE HOW FALSE EXPECTATIONS AND FANTASIES CAUSE SELF-DECEPTION AND BLINDNESS TO RED FLAGS

When we start dating someone, it's easy to get caught up in excitement. We start imagining what life could be like with this person. We dream about the future, thinking about what we *want* the relationship to be. But, if we let our imaginations and false hopes take over, we can miss the truth of who the person really is. We might ignore the **red flags**—the warning signs God gives us—because we're too busy chasing a fantasy. This leads to **self-deception** and sets us up for heartache.

This chapter will cover three things. First, why it's dangerous to let your imagination run wild in a relationship. Second, how false expectations can blind you. Third, the importance of noticing the red flags that God might be showing you. We'll also look at the Bible. It says to live in truth and trust God to guide us, not our emotions.

THE DANGER OF LETTING
YOUR IMAGINATION TAKE OVER

When you meet someone new and start feeling excited, it's easy to let your imagination run wild. You start dreaming about what your life together could look like. You think about getting married, having kids, and building a future with this person. It's fine to be hopeful about the future. But, it becomes dangerous if you imagine things that aren't real or expect someone to be what they're not.

I've seen this happen, ladies, where some of y'all are treating every little thing a man does like it's a sign he's ready to marry you. Listen, if you're overthinking every move and making it seem like he's proposing, **stop it!** You might be idolizing marriage, and it's making you seem delusional and could be pushing away good potential partners. You cannot allow imaginations and fantasies to control you.

The Bible warns us in Proverbs 12:11, "Those who work their land will have abundant food, but those who chase fantasies have no sense." In other words, people who focus on reality will succeed, but those who chase fantasies are not being wise. If we spend too much time dreaming and imagining, we can miss the truth of what's really happening in the relationship.

False hopes can make us believe the person will change. We may think we can "fix" their problems. Or we might think love will solve all our issues. But real love isn't built on fantasy—it's built on truth, honesty, and seeing things clearly. Ephesians 4:25 says, "Therefore, each of you must put off falsehood and speak truthfully to your neighbor, for we are all members of one body." If we aren't honest with ourselves and with the person we're dating, the relationship is built on lies.

SELF-DECEPTION: IGNORING RED FLAGS

When we let our emotions and imagination control us, we start ignoring the **red flags**. Red flags are warning signs that something isn't right in the relationship. These are God's way of protecting us from future pain. But when we're caught up in excitement or false expectations, we convince ourselves that the red flags don't matter or that they'll go away.

Here are some common red flags in relationships:

- **Inconsistent Faith:** The person claims to be a Christian, but their life doesn't reflect a real relationship with Jesus. Maybe they don't go to church, don't pray, or don't live according to biblical principles.
- **Disrespecting Boundaries:** They don't respect your boundaries, whether physical, emotional, or spiritual. This could include: pushing for intimacy before marriage, wasting your time, or crossing your boundaries.
- **Dishonesty or Manipulation:** They are not honest with you, or they try to control or manipulate situations to get their way.

- **Anger and Jealousy:** They get angry easily, are overly jealous, or try to control who you spend time with.

These are serious red flags, and if you see them, you need to pay attention. Don't ignore what God is trying to show you. Proverbs 27:12 says, "The prudent see danger and take refuge, but the simple keep going and pay the penalty." This means wise people see trouble coming and take action, but those who ignore the warning signs will suffer the consequences.

Ignoring red flags doesn't make them go away. If you're hoping that the person will change or that love will fix everything, you're deceiving yourself. God gives us wisdom to see things clearly, but we have to be willing to listen.

WHOLE DOES NOT MEAN PERFECT, BUT IT DOES MEAN HEALTHY

It's important to understand that **wholeness** does not mean you or the person you're dating has to be perfect. But you both need to be **healthy**—emotionally, mentally, and spiritually. Colossians 2:10 tells us, "In Christ, you have been brought to fullness." This means that we are made complete in Christ, not in a relationship with another person. If you or the person you're dating is not emotionally or spiritually healthy, the relationship will suffer.

Many people enter relationships thinking that their partner will "complete" them or fix what's broken inside of them. But no person can do that—only God can. When you're not whole, you end up putting pressure on the relationship and expecting your partner to fill a void that only God can fill.

It's important to be **whole in Christ** before you enter a relationship. This doesn't mean you have to be perfect, but it does mean you need to be healthy. You need to trust God to make you whole so that you're not looking to someone else to fix you. When both people are whole and healthy in Christ, the relationship will be built on a strong foundation.

SPEAKING TO WOMEN: GUARD YOUR HEART AND PAY ATTENTION

Sis, it's so easy to get caught up in your feelings and dreams about a relationship. You may want so badly for it to work out that you ignore the warning signs. But Proverbs 4:23 tells us, "Above all else, guard your heart, for everything you do flows from it." Guarding your heart means being careful about who you allow into your life and not letting your emotions blind you to the truth.

If you see red flags, don't ignore them. Pray and ask God for wisdom. Don't build your hopes on fantasies or expect the person to change. Be honest with yourself about who they are, and trust that God will guide you to the right person in His perfect timing.

SPEAKING TO MEN:
LEAD WITH TRUTH AND DISCERNMENT

Bro, God calls you to lead with wisdom and discernment, not with emotions or fantasies. As the leader in a relationship, you are responsible for building a strong, truthful foundation. Don't let your feelings blind you to the reality of the relationship. If there are red flags, it's your responsibility to take them seriously and seek God's guidance.

Ephesians 5:25 says, "Husbands, love your wives, just as Christ loved the church and gave Himself up for her." This means leading with selfless love, but it also means being truthful and wise. Don't build a relationship on wishful thinking or ignore warning signs that could lead to future problems.

PRACTICAL STEPS TO AVOID
SELF-DECEPTION AND FALSE EXPECTATIONS

1. **Pray for Discernment:** Ask God for wisdom as you enter into relationships. James 1:5 says, "If any of you lacks wisdom, you should ask God... and it will be given to you." Don't rely only on your emotions—ask God to help you see things clearly.

2. **Take Things Slowly:** Don't rush into a relationship or get emotionally involved too quickly. Take your time to get to know the person and pray for guidance before making any commitments.

3. **Seek Wise Counsel:** Proverbs 11:14 says, "For lack of guidance a nation falls, but victory is won through many

advisers." Talk to trusted mentors, pastors, or friends who can help you see things clearly. Sometimes others can see things that we miss.

4. **Look for the Fruit:** Jesus said in Matthew 7:16, "By their fruit you will recognize them." Pay attention to the person's actions, behaviors, and lifestyle. Are they living according to God's Word? Are they producing good fruit, or are there signs of trouble?

WHOLE IN CHRIST, NOT PERFECT, BUT HEALTHY

Remember, you don't have to be perfect to enter a relationship, but you do need to be **whole** in Christ. Trust God to heal any areas of brokenness in your heart before you seek love. When you are whole in Christ, you won't rely on someone else to make you complete, and you'll be able to enter a relationship from a place of strength and health. Pay attention to God's warnings, and don't let your imagination or emotions lead you into self-deception.

TIME OF REFLECTION

Take a moment to reflect on your past or current relationships. Ask yourself:

- Have I let my imagination or false expectations take control?
- Have I ignored red flags because I wanted the relationship to work?

- Am I seeking wholeness in Christ, or am I looking for someone else to complete me?
- What steps can I take to seek God's wisdom and build healthy relationships based on truth?

If you've been caught up in false expectations, now is the time to surrender them to God and ask Him to guide you in truth.

PRAYER FOR WISDOM AND DISCERNMENT

Lord, I ask for Your wisdom and guidance in my relationships. Help me to see things clearly and not be led by my emotions or false expectations. Open my eyes to any red flags and give me the strength to act on Your wisdom. Help me to trust in Your perfect plan for my life, knowing that You will guide me toward healthy, godly relationships. In Jesus' name, Amen.

I HATE HOW ONCE PEOPLE START DATING, THEY BEGIN TO NEGLECT FRIENDSHIPS AND COMMUNITY

A change happens when people start dating. They get so caught up in dating that they forget everything else. The friends who once mattered and their community have become an afterthought. They're so focused on the person they're dating that they push everyone else aside. It's easy to understand, but it's not healthy—and it's not how God intended us to live.

God designed us to live in **community**, to have people around us who love us, encourage us, and hold us accountable. Dating and shutting out your friends or community isolates you. You're cutting yourself off from the support system God gave you. Let me be clear: **you are not meant to date in isolation**. God calls us to build relationships within the body of Christ, not outside of it. Ignoring your community when you're dating can hurt you, your friendships, and your relationship.

This chapter will discuss the importance of staying connected to your friends and community, even when in a relationship. You'll learn about the risks of dating in isolation. You'll also learn why God wants you to stay in fellowship with other believers. If you've been pushing your friends and community aside for your relationship, it's time to bring things back into balance.

THE TRAP OF DATING IN ISOLATION

The thrill of a new romance can be intoxicating. You're drawn to spend every moment with your newfound love, neglecting other relationships. Yet this all-consuming focus poses risks. Gradually, you may find yourself drifting from friends and faith community. New love must balance with existing connections. Don't lose sight of your life. Without even realizing it, you've slipped into **isolation**.

God never intended for us to live in isolation. He created us to be in relationships with other people—our friends, our family, and our church. Ecclesiastes 4:9-10 reminds us, "Two are better than one, because they have a good return for their labor: If either of them falls down, one can help the other up." If you isolate yourself from your friends and community, who will be there to help you when you fall?

Dating in isolation is risky. You lose the support, wisdom, and accountability of a healthy community. Your friends and church family are the ones who can see things you might miss or purposely choose to ignore. They can give you godly advice and help you make wise decisions. Proverbs 11:14 says, "Where there is no guidance, a people falls, but in an abundance of counselors there is safety." When you cut yourself off from community, you're cutting yourself off from the very people God placed in your life to help guide you.

WHY COMMUNITY MATTERS IN DATING

God created us to live in **community**, not just when we're single, but in every season of life—including dating. Here's why community is so important when you're in a relationship:

1. **Accountability and Wisdom:** Your friends and church family can give you wise advice and hold you accountable as you date. They might notice red flags or point out areas where you need to set better boundaries. Proverbs 27:17 says, "As iron sharpens iron, so one person sharpens another." Your friends help sharpen you and make you better, but they can't do that if you shut them out.

2. **Spiritual Growth:** Being in a church community keeps you growing in your faith. When you're dating, it's easy to become so focused on your relationship that you stop focusing on God. Staying involved in your church helps keep your spiritual life strong. Hebrews 10:24-25 says, "Let us consider how we may spur one another on toward love and good deeds, not giving up meeting together." Don't stop meeting with other believers just because you're in a relationship.

3. **Support During Tough Times:** Relationships aren't always easy, and there will be times when you need

encouragement and prayer. Your friends and church family are there to support you when things get hard. Galatians 6:2 says, "Carry each other's burdens, and in this way, you will fulfill the law of Christ." Don't try to carry your relationship struggles alone—let your community help you.

4. **Balance in Life:** Your friends and community help keep your life balanced. It's important to invest in your romantic relationship, but it shouldn't be the only relationship that matters. God wants you to have a well-rounded life, filled with friendships, service to others, and growing in your walk with Him. Ephesians 4:16 says, "From him the whole body, joined and held together by every supporting ligament, grows and builds itself up in love." Your community helps you grow, and you need them just as much as they need you.

THE DANGERS OF IDOLIZING YOUR RELATIONSHIP

Neglecting your friendships and church can lead to idolizing your relationship. That's one of the biggest dangers. When you spend all your time focused on your partner, you risk making that person the most important thing in your life—even more important than God. This is a form of **idolatry**, and it's dangerous.

Exodus 20:3 says, "You shall have no other gods before me." That includes your relationship. No matter how much you love the person you're dating, they can never take the place of God in your life. When you put your relationship above everything else, you're missing the bigger picture of what God wants for you.

Your relationship should be a **blessing from God**, but it should never pull you away from God or His people. Matthew 6:33 tells us, "But seek first his kingdom and his righteousness, and all these things will be given to you as well." When you put God first, everything else—including your relationship—will fall into place.

DON'T DATE IN ISOLATION – STAY CONNECTED TO COMMUNITY

Dating in isolation may seem good at first, as it focuses on building your relationship. However, it can harm you in the long run. You need your community—friends, church family, and fellow believers. They offer wisdom, support, and accountability, which are vital for a healthy relationship.

Isolating yourself can lead to spiritual weakness. Without a community, you might follow emotions over God's truth. This can lead to compromising values, pushing limits, or drifting from faith. So, staying connected to your church and friends while dating is crucial.

Hebrews 10:24-25 says, "Let's inspire each other to love and good deeds. Don't stop meeting together, as some do. Instead, encourage each other." God wants us to stay connected with other believers. This is not just for our own benefit, but also to help each other grow.

SPEAKING TO WOMEN:
KEEP YOUR FRIENDSHIPS STRONG

Sis, I get it. When you start dating someone, it's easy to get wrapped up in the relationship. But don't forget about the friends who have been there for you all along. Your friends are a source of wisdom, support, and love, and they will be there for you when things get tough. Don't shut them out just because you're focused on your relationship.

Keep your friendships strong. Make time for your friends, and don't neglect your church family. They are a gift from God, and you need them just as much as they need you.

SPEAKING TO MEN: DON'T ISOLATE YOURSELF

Bro, it's easy to think that when you're dating, you need to focus only on that one relationship. But God didn't call you to isolate yourself. You need your friends and church family to keep you grounded, hold you accountable, and encourage you in your walk with Christ.

Stay connected to your community. Don't let your relationship be the only thing that matters in your life. God has a bigger plan for you, and He's placed people in your life to help you grow and stay on the right path.

BIBLICAL PRINCIPLES FOR STAYING CONNECTED
TO COMMUNITY WHILE DATING

Here are some key biblical principles to remember when it comes to staying connected to your community while dating:

1. **Value Friendships:** Proverbs 17:17 says, "A friend loves at all times, and a brother is born for a time of adversity." Cherish your friendships, especially when you're in a relationship. Your friends are there for you in both good times and bad.

2. **Stay Involved in Your Church:** Don't neglect meeting together with other believers. Hebrews 10:25 reminds us to keep meeting with our church family to encourage one another and grow together in our faith.

3. **Seek God First:** Matthew 6:33 tells us to seek God's kingdom first. Your relationship is important, but it should never take priority over your relationship with God. Keep Him first in everything.

4. **Stay Accountable:** Proverbs 27:17 reminds us that iron sharpens iron. Stay accountable to your friends and community, and let them help guide you in your relationship decisions.

RELATIONSHIPS ARE MEANT TO GROW IN COMMUNITY

God designed relationships to grow and flourish within the context of community. Don't isolate yourself when you start dating—stay connected to your friends, your church family, and most importantly, to God. Healthy relationships are built on a foundation of strong community, accountability, and spiritual growth. Keep balance in your life, and trust God to guide you in your relationship.

TIME OF REFLECTION

Take a moment to reflect on your relationships. Ask yourself:

- Have I been neglecting my friends or my church since I started dating?
- Am I still seeking God first in my relationship?
- How can I stay connected to my community while building my relationship?

If any of these questions reveal areas where you've become too isolated, now is the time to make changes. Stay connected, stay grounded, and trust God to lead you.

PRAYER FOR BALANCE IN RELATIONSHIPS

Lord, I ask for Your wisdom as I navigate my relationships. Help me to stay connected to my community, to keep my friendships strong, and to put You first in everything. Guard my heart from isolating myself and help me to live in the balance You've called me to. Guide my relationship and help it to grow within the context of healthy friendships and church family. In Jesus' name, Amen.

LET GOD LEAD YOUR RELATIONSHIPS, AND TRUST HIS PLAN

As we come to the end of this book, there's one central truth that I want you to take with you: **God has a plan for your love life**. His plan is far better than anything you can imagine or create on your own. But to experience the fullness of that plan, you have to trust Him, follow His principles, and let Him lead every step of the way.

Throughout these chapters, we've explored many reasons why cultural dating practices often lead to heartbreak, confusion, and sin. We've talked about the pressures to conform, the dangers of emotional and physical compromise, and the importance of setting boundaries. We've discussed how ignoring red flags, dating with unhealed wounds, and neglecting community can hurt you and your relationship. All of these pitfalls come from trying to do things **our own way** instead of God's way.

But here's the good news: **God's way is the BEST Way!** His principles for dating, relationships, and marriage are designed to protect you, bless you, and bring you joy. When you follow His plan—by seeking Him first, maintaining your integrity, and staying connected to your community—your relationships will flourish in ways you never thought possible. Even if you've made mistakes in the past, it's never too late to turn back to God and ask Him to guide your path from this point forward.

LET GOD WRITE YOUR LOVE STORY

If there's one piece of advice I can leave you with, it's this: **let God write your love story.** So many of us try to take control of our relationships, rushing ahead without waiting on God's timing. We get caught up in emotions, desires, and fantasies, and we end up disappointed when things don't work out the way we hoped. I remember feeling so frustrated when people tried to encourage me with advice I didn't want to hear. I was stubborn and determined to write my own love story. Deep down, I thought I knew what was best for my life. I didn't say it out loud, but in my heart, I believed I could handle things better than God could. That decision cost me **everything**. My life was completely derailed. And the worst part? In chasing my own will instead of God's, I unintentionally hurt one of the most important people in my life—my daughter.

Because I wanted my own way, my daughter will never know what it's like to wake up every day in a home with both her biological mom and dad. No matter how much we explain that it wasn't her fault and tell her how much we love her, she still has to live with the confusion and the pain of wondering why we aren't together. Every day, she battles the weight of feeling like she has to choose between her parents. I see the struggle in her eyes, and no words can completely heal the wound that comes from a broken family.

I could go on and on about the impact of my choices, but I say this to **warn you: STOP treating dating like a game.** It's not something to take lightly. Look at my life and learn from my mistakes. Yes, the Lord is a restorer, and He has redeemed so much in my life, but I still carry the weight of the consequences of my actions. I wanted what I wanted, and I ignored God's warnings. I thought I was the exception, thinking, "I won't become a single mom. That won't be me." But it *was* me.

God has been so merciful, and He restored me, but this doesn't have to be your story. You can choose differently. Look at my husband's life—he trusted God, waited for His timing, and because of his obedience, he avoided so much unnecessary pain and suffering. The Lord blessed him with a love story that honors Him, and it spared him from the heartache I endured. **You don't have to go through what I went through.** Choose God's way, trust His plan, and save yourself from the weight of unnecessary consequences.

When you **surrender your love life to God,** He will work in ways that exceed your expectations. Ephesians 3:20 tells us, "Now to him who is able to do immeasurably more than all we ask or imagine, according to his power that is at work within us." God knows your heart, your desires, and your future, and He has a perfect plan for your relationships.

When I look back on my own journey, I realize that I had to come to a point where I trusted God fully with my love life. I had made mistakes, experienced heartbreak, and struggled with feelings of loneliness and frustration. But when I finally let go and allowed God to take control, He brought healing to my heart and led me to a relationship that honors Him. Now, I'm happily married with five beautiful children, but it all began with surrendering my dating life to Him.

TRUST GOD WITH YOUR HEALING

For many of you, the journey to healthy relationships will begin with healing. We've talked about how **unhealed wounds from** past relationships, trauma, or childhood can affect your dating life. If you're still carrying pain, insecurity, or fear, I encourage you to let God heal your heart before you step into a relationship. Only God can truly make you whole.

Psalm 147:3 says, "He heals the brokenhearted and binds up their wounds." If you've been hurt, rejected, or left feeling broken, remember that God is your Healer. He can take the pain of your past and turn it into a testimony of His grace. But healing takes time, and it takes a willingness to face your wounds and let God work in your heart. Don't rush the process—let God make you whole so that you can enter a relationship from a place of strength and health.

DON'T DATE TO CONVERT, DON'T DATE IN ISOLATION

Two important things to remember as you move forward in your relationships: **don't date to convert someone**, and **don't date in isolation**.

First, you cannot change or "fix" someone through a relationship. If the person you're interested in doesn't share your faith or isn't truly committed to following Jesus, don't assume that dating them will bring them closer to God. 2 Corinthians 6:14 reminds us, "Do not be yoked together with unbelievers. For what do righteousness and wickedness have in common?" You deserve to be with someone who shares your faith and values, so trust God to bring the right person into your life.

Second, don't isolate yourself from your friends, family, and church community when you start dating. As we've discussed, dating in isolation can lead to a lack of accountability and cause you to lose touch with the people who are there to support you. Proverbs 11:14 says, "Where there is no counsel, the people fall; but in the multitude of counselors there is safety." Keep your friendships strong, stay connected to your church, and let your community help you grow in your relationship.

HOLINESS IS THE FOUNDATION

One thing we've come back to over and over again is the importance of **holiness** in dating. The world's way of dating often leads to physical and emotional compromise, but God calls us to a higher standard. 1 Peter 1:16 reminds us, "Be holy, because I am holy." Holiness isn't just about following rules—it's about living a life that reflects God's love, purity, and grace.

When you pursue holiness in your relationships, you're setting yourself up for God's best. You're protecting your heart, guarding your boundaries, and honoring God in everything you do. This doesn't mean you'll be perfect, but it means you're committed to living in a way that pleases God and brings Him glory.

Remember Too much time, Too much Talk, and Too Much Touch will lead you into fornication. It's important to stay **S.A.F.E.** by guarding your heart and maintaining healthy boundaries. If you apply this

THE S.A.F.E. RULE:

To keep your heart and purity safe while dating, remember the **S.A.F.E.** Rule:

1. **S: Spending Too Much Time** – Be careful not to spend all your time together too soon, as it can make you feel closer than you really are.
2. **A: Avoid Sharing Too Many Secrets** – Sharing too much too fast can create emotional closeness that isn't meant to happen yet.
3. **F: Physical Feelings** – Getting physically close (like hugging or holding hands) can lead to bigger temptations and cross boundaries.

4. **E: Emotional Intimacy** – Being too emotionally attached can cause you to ignore important things in a relationship and lead to heartache.

The **S.A.F.E.** Rule helps you protect yourself from rushing into emotional and physical closeness, keeping your relationship on the right path.

TAKE IT ONE STEP AT A TIME

If you've been overwhelmed by the challenges of dating or feel discouraged by past mistakes, I want to encourage you: **take it one step at a time**. God isn't asking you to have everything figured out right now. He simply wants you to trust Him, follow His lead, and make decisions that align with His Word.

Proverbs 3:5-6 says, "Trust in the Lord with all your heart and lean not on your own understanding; in all your ways submit to him, and he will make your paths straight." Take each step of your dating journey with Him by your side. He will guide you, protect you, and lead you to the right person in His perfect timing.

SURRENDER AND TRUST

As we close this journey together, remember that your love life is not something you have to figure out on your own. **Jesus Christ is your guide**, and He is faithful to lead you when you surrender your heart and trust His plan. Don't rush ahead, don't settle for less than God's best, and don't let the world's way of dating distract you from the beauty of doing it God's way.

**Let God write your love story.
His way is better, His timing is perfect, and
His love is greater than anything you could ever imagine.**

PRAYER OF SURRENDER

Dear Lord, I thank You for the lessons I've learned throughout this journey. I surrender my love life to You, trusting that Your plan is far better than anything I could imagine. Heal the areas of my heart that are still hurting, and help me walk in purity and wisdom as I pursue relationships. Guide me in Your truth, and help me wait on Your perfect timing. I trust You to bring the right person into my life and to lead me in a relationship that honors You. In Jesus' name, Amen.

NOTES

Jones, A. K. (1996). God's design for women: An exploration of the Pauline Epistles' passages on the role of women: An honors thesis (HONRS 499). https://core.ac.uk/download/5009415.pdf

Twenty-Fifth Day of Lenten Reflection: "Let your light shine before others". https://www.christianityinfo.com/2024/01/twenty-fifth-day-of-lenten-reflection.html

Embrace the Freedom of Grace: God's Redemption At Christ's Expense, Rejecting Legalism and Lawlessness -. https://operationtransform.org/embrace-the-freedom-of-grace-gods-redemption-at-christs-expense-rejecting-legalism-and-lawlessness/

Joyce Meyer: How To Be Pure In Heart - ALL PASTORS. https://www.allpastors.com/joyce-meyer-how-to-be-pure-in-heart/